Lavender & Old Ladies

A Collection of Non-Fiction

Edited by Kevin Zazzali

Lavender
& Old Ladies

A Collection of Non-Fiction

Edited by Kevin Zazzali

Apprentice House
Baltimore, Maryland
www.apprenticehouse.com

13-Digit ISBN: 978-1-934074-09-1

Printed in the United States of America

First Edition

Published by Apprentice House
The Future of Publishing...Today!

Project Manager & Senior Editor: Kevin Zazzali
Associate Editor: Julia Sherrier
Assistant Editor: Jerrell Cameron
Cover design by Kimberly Schurtz

Apprentice House
Communication Department
Loyola College in Maryland
4501 N. Charles Street
Baltimore, MD 21210

410.617.5265 • 410.617.5040 (fax)
www.ApprenticeHouse.com
info@ApprenticeHouse.com

Contents

Preface

Kevin Zazzali, editor

Forum has been a place for Loyola College students to showcase their passion for writing non-fiction as far back as 1979. Selected pieces of the *Forum* have been assembled into this compilation – timeless stories ranging from such topics as racism to multiculturalism; from living with AIDS to dying from AIDS; from quantum physics to existentialism; from Esperanto to terrorism; from the respect for history to the fears of growing up; and from living with obsessive-compulsive disorder to dying from cancer. Readers will be hard-pressed to determine whether a story was written in 1986 or 2006. Therein lies the beauty of *Lavender & Old Ladies*: its content has a degree of timelessness.

These short stories are all true. The characters are all real. The emotions driving these works will grip the hearts and minds of readers for years to come. I gain much pleasure from the idea that readers will be able to discover how alumni found themselves through writing. These stories do not necessarily offer any answers to life's big questions, but they offer readers a small glimpse into the lives of past Loyola students at a time when they were attempting to discover who they were and what their place was in this world.

Introduction

Barbara Mallonee

In January 2007, *Forum Magazine* marks its thirtieth anniversary at Loyola College. I think it is wonderful that *Forum* has a history long enough to warrant restrospection – and surely the College that has underwritten its production for three decades should be pleased that Kevin Zazzali has created a collection of essays from *Forum*.

The pieces in this new collection are chosen from the second half of *Forum's* thirty-year run – Spring 1991 through Fall 2005. *Forum* actually grew in three stages:

The first three volumes (January 1977, Spring 1979, Winter 1980) were typed (using a Royal typewriter!) on legal-size paper, mimeographed, folded and stapled together by writing faculty under the leadership of Xav (Francis Xavier) Trainor, who had been hired in 1971 to direct freshman writing.

The next twelve volumes (Spring 1981-Spring 1988) were planned by a small *Forum* staff advised by me and printed at the College's "central duplicating" facility in brown ink on ivory with cover artwork done by the editors (though in 1982, we resorted to using a kitchen sponge to print a circle that would match an epigraph from E. B. White's essay "The Ring of Time"!).

In 1989, *Forum* took a quantum leap; its new faculty moderator was Daniel McGuiness, and, for the first time, the magazine was produced by an off-campus professional printer. Perfect-bound with a handsome glossy cover, sixteen pieces of art, quotations from famous writers spaced throughout, and even biographies of its "contributers" at the end, the 100-page volume was produced by a large staff – its editor Kathleen Klaus, two assistants to the editor, an art director, layout production and publicity staff members, and a ten-person strong prose board. In conjunction with its production, there was a student reading.

The shift from faculty advisor to faculty moderator was significant. Dan McGuiness saw his job as three-fold: to choose an editor for *Forum*, to hand that editor a few winning essays from the department's writing contest for inclusion in the magazine – and, ten months later, to help the editor deliver text to the printer whose payment by the Dean's office Dan arranged. Dan's office door was always open, and editor, staff and writers stopped by often for encouragement and advice and praise, but to the students went choices and decisions as they met to gather additional essays, edit and arrange them, invite and select artwork, choose typeface, and proofread. At its side (and also on its side in rare moments of controversy or dispute), Dan stood and let *Forum* become autonomous.

Still, this coming of age as an independent literary magazine was the logical outgrowth of the premise for the magazine in the first place. I still have that first volume of *Forum* with its pale blue cover with the Evergreen logo on the back – though it wasn't yet called *Forum*. Its title: **LOYOLA STUDENTS <u>DO</u> LEARN TO WRITE.** The title sounds pedantic, but, in context, the title was neither offensive nor defensive. The magazine was directed not to the academic community nor to the general public, but to each and every student who had taken CA113 Effective Writing the previous semester with faculty whose enthusiasm for their writing was already legendary! The statement was celebratory!

The magazine was only eight pages long – and two of those pages were taken up with a letter written by Xav Trainor "to all students in Effective Writing":

"...let us now make one general observation that we could not afford to make during the course. As you well know, there is no other single academic subject that receives more attention in newspapers, magazines and journals than writing. And you are familiar with the general lament: students today cannot write, be they high school, undergraduate, or graduate students. Although we do not know firsthand what the situation is on other campuses in the country (we could make a good guess), we do know that here at Loyola our students can and do learn to write – and write well. In that regard we think Loyola students are not typical. If that is true, and we offer support in this booklet to show that it is, we think that what makes you different is your willingness to apply yourselves to the very arduous kind of work that writing demands, despite all the understandable excuses you could have used to avoid it. We offer this generality in all sincerity, not to flatter but to reassure you (as we said so many times in class) that as discouraging and as frustrating and as threatening as a writing course may be, you can learn to think logically, support your thinking concretely, and express your thought in literate language if you will simply perservere. Let the proof of that important generality rest on these few – but typical – sample papers that we send back to you in this booklet."

Xav Trainor believed that those who <u>can</u> write should be called *writers*. His admiration for those who would cast the personal into prose ran from Teilhard de Chardin and Elie Weisel (Xav brought him to Loyola to speak to our students) to our *Forum* writers – Matthew McKenna, who in 1979 wrote "Nietzsche, Sartre and Kierkegaard on God and Freedom," Patrick Curran, who wrote in 1980 on Don McLean's *American Pie*, and Karen Wilson, who in 1981 wrote on waitressing as does Carlene Bauer in "Self du Jour" in this new collection. From the department's inception in the early 70's, the writing faculty determined that our students would become not only experts in a discipline but also writers – in real fields and real genres. By the time Dan McGuiness professionalized *Forum,* we already had in place a twelve-year history of publishing young writers whom their faculty took seriously, convinced that they had language and life experiences and learning enough to join the ranks of American essayists.

The essay is a genre that has flourished in this country! No anthology fails to honor essayists abroad – Seneca , Francis Bacon, Michel de Montaigne, George Orwell and Virginia Woolf – but ever since Emerson, the essay has been a form of American art. In the space of two centuries, the essay has caught the rhythms of high, low and popular culture, filling the pages of magazines, literary journals, and the wide-open op-ed spaces of our nation's newspapers. How many essays have been written – and published, might we suppose? *Forum* alone has published 372 essays. Hefty collections of essays fill the shelves of bookstores – in the nonfiction section, of course, but also in areas like nature, science, travel, cooking, religion, philosophy, parenting and pets. Since 1986, Robert Atwan has edited with a guest essayist an annual series of "best American essays," and the range of writers and venues is wide.

On my desk on this summer afternoon is a full collection of *Forum Magazine* (32 issues, no two alike in design or even size), this proposed Apprentice House typescript of *Forum* essays, and a copy of *The Best American Essays 2005,* edited by Louis Menand, in which appears a *New Yorker* essay by Jonathan Franzen titled "Caught." It's one of the best essays for young people I think I have ever read, and I consider it significant that, measured against the Franzen essay, all the essays in *Lavender & Old Ladies* hold their own.

"Essays," wrote Edward Hoagland in 1976, "are directly concerned with the mind and the mind's idiosyncrasy...and the fascination of the mind is the fascination of the essay."

The essays in this collection are all over the map in terms of subject matter. They have in common the features that distinguish all good essays. They have an original idea that responds to a genuine pulse of curiosity, joy, outrage, empathy, hilarity or sorrow. In this collection, writers explore everything from events in their own life ("Waking Up to the Bomb") to the experience of friends ("Crossword Puzzles and M & M's") to research into the minds of strangers ("Dust of the Ground"), into remote places ("Art of Living: Give and Take"), even into historic figures ("From Gravity to God"). Most important is the gifted use of language. "Essays don't usually boil down to a summary, as articles do," Hoagland reminds writers, "and the style of the writer has a 'nap' to it, a combination of personality and originality and energetic loose ends that stand up like the nap on a piece of wool and can't be brushed flat." These essays are nuanced and lively.

I do and I don't understand the title of this collection. In keeping with convention, *Lavender & Old Ladies* is the title of an essay in the collection. I grow lavender; I grow old; the title strikes a chord with me. But this collection is intended for newer, younger readers. Might not Peter

Blair's *Plop!* have been better? Then again, as I page through the typescript, I am touched that though my generation is alternately appalled and astounded by youth, when push comes to shove in these essays, it is from encounters with parents, grandparents, aunts, uncles, teachers, mentors and strangers that young people write. They do not look to old ladies and older gentlemen to pass on wisdom (youth creates its own code), but generations have always clashed and clung, and these young writers recognize their forebears and elders as people who touch their lives, who touch their hearts, who shape and shade their minds – as touchstones as life swirls by. The tenor of the encounter is sometimes sweet, sometimes savage, but always for the writers, the encounter is for better, not for worse.

Revamped, the 1989 *Forum* with its pale blue cover opened with words from Walt Whitman: "A perfect writer would make words sing, dance, kiss, do the male and female act, bear children, weep, bleed, rage, stab, steal, fire cannons, steer ships, sack cities..." The essays in this collection are the work of "perfect writers."

One final thought. Just as Dan McGuiness stepped back in 1989, trusting students to take charge of *Forum,* so too from these essays has vanished any trace of the faculty members who helped the students to write. All praise for these essays belongs to the writers, taught to ply their craft. And yet, I have to say (though strictly as an aside) that this collection does Xav Trainor (who inspired so many) and Dan McGuiness and a continuous stream of dedicated Loyola faculty proud.

Barbara C. Mallonee
Associate Professor, Department of Writing
Loyola College in Maryland

August 2006

Pictures of My Mother

Jason Santalucia
Spring 1991 – Volume XII

On this warm October afternoon, I came home from my classes excited about something that had happened that day. I don't remember what exactly, but I wanted to share it with someone, and my mother was the only person home. Setting my bag of texts and notebooks down by the steps, I saw a light under the basement door and walked down to the laundry room where she was sorting clothes into lights and darks, separating them into limp, drooping piles on the cement floor. Her round face was expressionless as she worked in the glare of a naked light bulb, her tiny mouth shut tight, until she screamed and clawed the shirt she was holding as she finally noticed me. She hadn't heard me come in.

"Hi," I mumbled.

"Don't do that again."

"Sorry." I waited a moment for her to say something, start a conversation, but she didn't, only went back to her business. Thoughts of subtle ways to bring up my news came to my mind, but I finally chose the blunt course and blurted it out. I suppose I expected her to gush over me and make a big deal out of it, the way she had when I was little and would do something stupid like make a crayon picture of stick men for her, or do a cannonball into a swimming pool. Look mom, look! Her reaction was flat, tough, the way I half expected it to be.

"Oh, God, how much is that going to cost?" she whined, never taking her eyes from the sock she was pushing into a neat little ball. In one line, she took me from excitement to feeling like a brat and a fool.

"Jesus Christ, Dorothy," I said in a flat tone and walked out. These words had been chosen specifically to anger and hurt my mother because I knew they would cross two lines that exist within her. The first was simply that my mother is very religious and, to take the name of the Lord in vain like that, I knew, would infuriate her. Calling her by her mother's name, Dorothy, though, was crueler than breaking any commandment, and this I knew as well.

"Don't ever call me that," she shouted up the steps after me, but I was already gone.

My mother wears a sad expression in every childhood picture I've ever seen of her. It's the eyes that do it. Huge brown eyes that seem ready to well over, set among pale, delicate features; a sharp nose and pinched, narrow lips. Her head, with its straight brown hair, seems almost out of proportion to her tiny body, always dressed in a plain dress, invariably made by my grandmother. When she talks of her childhood, my mother always speaks in hushed tones and stares, trance-like, across the room, at what I can only guess.

Sarah Suzanne Mentzer was born on November 27, 1944, in a small hospital in the Oakmont section of Pittsburgh. She was the daughter of Walter Mentzer, a mason, and his wife of nearly twenty years at the time, Dorothy Kreamer Mentzer. She had one brother, Walter, nicknamed Wattie, who was six years her senior, and a sister, Minah Jeanine, shortened to Miney, who was sixteen years her senior. From all external appearances, theirs was a happy, normal life. They lived in a meticulously neat house in a pleasant section of the town, attended the local

Lutheran church, and got along well with their neighbors. Inside the house, though, my mother remembers a different reality.

"Your grandfather would come home drunk almost every night, and then it would start," my mother tells me. "It" was the fighting between my uncle, then in his teens, and my grandfather. They would start like children, my grandfather calling my uncle names and making fun of his size, though he was only average at best himself. He knew my uncle's sensitivity in this area, knew how he lifted weights furiously, grunts and strained breathing coming up the basement steps every afternoon, but to no end, he was always a small boy, short and thin with narrow shoulders. Then would come the accusations of laziness. "Why don't you get a job, you're almost out of school and don't know a damn thing," he'd stammer as he bumped his way through the house, following the boy. This was not entirely true, though, because my uncle did have two skills, which he uses to this day. He knew something about cars and a lot about people.

"I doubt if Wattie even knows how many cars he's owned in his lifetime," my mother explains to me. "He used to buy a car, clean it up, sometimes do no more than wash and wax it, and then sell it and make hundreds." My uncle, even as a teenager, could play people. He'd tell them he'd had the car for years, had rebuilt it from the frame up and was only selling it because he was going into the service to defend his country from the Communists. America and red engine paint, the best car salesmen known.

Uncle Wattie also knew how to play my grandfather. "You're drunk and you stink," he'd say, forcing a condescending laugh. Then he'd start to push him, not hard, but just enough to tip his swaggering frame off balance, and send my grandfather crashing into a table or lamp. It was more insult than physical attack, meant to illustrate just how incompetent the old man was. Just as he was financially incompetent. Wattie would ask why my grandmother had to pay all of the bills. "Because you'd piss your whole check away in one night," he'd answer himself, and then push my grandfather, who was struggling to gain his balance, back to the floor. Soon the pushes turned to punches, and the two, locked together, would go spinning through the kitchen or tiny living room as if they were dancing partners. "I don't know how long they'd go on like that," my mother tells me, "but eventually Wattie would usually end up running out of the house and squealing away in whatever hot rod he happened to have that week, then Daddy would start with me."

Worn from the fighting and the alcohol spinning in his head, my grandfather would drop himself into his chair and flick on the television, but not really to watch it. Instead he would start making fun of my mother, who, all the while, had been silently curled up on the couch. She forced herself not to cry, not while the shouting and fighting had been going on, and not now as her father sat heavily, telling her she was homely and probably retarded too. She knew that her crying would only give the man, with spit bubbling in the corners of his mouth, another reason to attack her. "He never hit me, though, I will say that, and eventually he'd pass out and lie there, stinking. Whiskey made him smell the worst; it came through his feet."

What my grandmother was doing at these times is not clear; my mother never says. In modern babble, I suppose she was the enabler; cooking, cleaning, and keeping her mouth shut. In fact, though, in its own way, this silence from my grandmother was as painful to my mother as the shouting of my grandfather. "I never felt loved," my mother says, while talking about her mother, "never felt loved at all."

My grandmother is a woman who believes in survival as a purely physical concept. If you have enough food and a warm place to sleep, then you are surviving. Indeed, most of her life was occupied by the work and worry of providing these basic necessities, first for herself, and then for her family. I know little of my grandmother's childhood, only what my mother tells me, which is, that the Kreamer family was quite large and quite poor. There is also a single photograph of my great-grandmother. It is a grainy, brown and white portrait of a large woman, staring dead straight into the camera. Her face is round and plain, just beginning to sag, with the thin hair pulled back tightly. The eyes are tiny, but intense, and the lipless mouth shows neither smile nor frown, simply a severe horizontal slash.

When my grandmother was fifteen, she married my grandfather, and soon after, the Depression hit. When I ask about this period, my grandfather only sighs and shakes his head. "We did alright, though, we're here today," my grandmother adds. Indeed, they did just that, alright. There always seemed to be a room that needed to be plastered or a foundation that needed to be laid some-place, and in this way, job-to-job, they pulled through. By the time my mother was born, they were becoming quite comfortable. In fact, my grandfather was by then partners with another man, Ted Bothel, in owning a small construction company, which he later lost because of his drinking. Still though, my grandmother found little, if any, time to indulge her youngest daughter. Strictness and regularity were the rules. There were no trips to the zoo or to the movies and no afternoons spent shopping, except once a week for groceries. Clothes were a waste when you could make them yourself. My grandmother's life revolved around maintaining her household. Every day was assigned a certain task so as to most efficiently accomplish this goal. A certain day was for cleaning the bathroom, another day for grocery shopping, another for dusting and cleaning, and still another for scrubbing the kitchen floor. "Every Friday we had chili for dinner," my mother remembers, "because it was easy, she could just let it simmer all day while she did the laundry. Friday was laundry day." In this way, my grandmother kept herself busy. There was always something to do. So much in fact, that she rarely left the house. To this day, she does not even have a driver's license.

I suppose that from her perspective, my grandmother did everything she was supposed to do to be a good mother to her little girl. Like a checklist, she could have gone down the line to assure herself of this. The child ate well, although quite blandly, strictly meat and potatoes and, of course, chili, had decent clothes, received a clean report from the doctor once a year, and had a comfortable home. Anything else would have been frivolous. Never mind the fact that my mother hated her home and felt no love from her parents. "I can remember never being allowed to bring friends home from school, but I didn't care because I would have been ashamed to anyway."

My mother's relationship with my Uncle Wattie was not very good either. "He used to tease me all the time, constantly, until I'd cry, and even then he'd keep going." One of my uncle's favorite taunts was telling his little sister that she had been adopted. "This made sense to me," my mother explains, chewing her lip. "All my friends' parents were much younger than mine, so I always believed Wattie when he'd tell me this, and he knew it because I'd always cry."

There were a couple of people, however, whom my mother loved and felt love from in return. One was my Aunt Miney. Although she had married my Uncle Bob, a huge, broad man, and moved out when my mother was still quite young, Aunt Miney remained in Pittsburgh and in touch with her sister, for whom she seemed to have a motherly love. I have no solid facts on which to base this feeling about my aunt's maternal love for my mother, only a single photograph, creased and faded. It is of Aunt Miney, in her early twenties, thin and quite attractive in a white skirt and a light sweater, kneeling down, with my mother sitting in her lap, holding a doll. Though there is no sky showing, only trees and bushes in the background, it appears to have been a sunny day as both sisters are squinting out from the picture. Perhaps it is simply their grins or the difference in their ages, I am not sure, but that photo does suggest to me, a bond other than that of sister to sister.

The other person my mother felt loved by was a nurse my grandmother had become good friends with while in the hospital for pneumonia. Pete, a nickname taken from her last name, Peters, was more of a friend to my mother than just an adult. She took time to talk to this little girl, and, more importantly, to listen to her. This is all that I know about Pete, though, because my mother never goes into detail, only smiles slightly and tells me, "I loved her." I suppose that is all I need to know.

To me, my mother seems to have gone from being a little girl to a grown woman, almost overnight, and with no years in between. She never talks of her adolescence, except for briefly mentioning the names of one or two of her old boyfriends once. Even the photographic record makes it seem as though she dropped from the earth during this period. Except for a couple of high school yearbook snapshots, the family photos begin with her baby pictures and go up until she was around ten, then stop, and begin again in her early twenties, around the time she met my father. In these latter photos there seems to have been a change in her. She had gone from a plain, mousy looking girl, to a very attractive young woman. It is the difference in her expressions, though, that is most striking. In the more recent photos, for the first time, I see my mother wearing a full, unrestrained smile in every picture. She appears genuine and quite happy, and I wonder if it is because she had simply learned to fake it and smile along, or if something had changed at home.

When I think of how my grandparents are today, though, I can't help believing that there had actually been a change, or at least the beginning of one, because the people I know as my grandparents do not fit the descriptions that my mother gives of her parents. It is as if a shift of power has taken place between them. Where once my grandfather appears to have been an unchallenged tyrant, today things now appear relatively equal, or perhaps a bit tipped toward my grandmother, as she is certainly no longer one to keep her mouth shut.

I can think of many times when I have personally witnessed my grandmother exert this power over her old and worn husband in the form of, for lack of a better phrase, incessant bitching. They bicker constantly; the slightest thing will set them off. Actually, though, I should have said the slightest thing will set her off, because these arguments are almost always very one-sided, with my grandmother yelling at, or complaining about, my grandfather, who just sits quietly, flipping cards in a seemingly endless game of solitaire, and only occasionally muttering something under his breath.

There is, however, one incident of my grandfather showing his old self, which remains quite clear in my memory. First, though, I should mention that my grandparents no longer live in Pittsburgh. About fifteen years ago, they moved to a small house in James Creek, which is nothing more than a rural postal route along a dirt road cutting across a mountain in central Pennsylvania. I mention this because an eleven year-old boy hacking at weeds with a machete might seem out of place in a city, but in James Creek, this is about the most interesting thing I could find to do. That is also how I managed to cut a deep gash in my leg. The tip of the blade had gone straight through my shorts and deep into my thigh. It bled heavily, so much so that I was afraid to look down, and instead, immediately limped back to the house where I stood in the kitchen, dazed, staring at my grandmother and dripping onto the floor. At first she thought it was a joke. "It didn't look like blood," she explained later. "There was too much, and it looked black." She soon realized it was no joke. "As soon as I looked at the cut," she tells me, "I knew you'd need stitches." As soon as I looked down at the cut, laid wide open with yellow globs of fat bulging into the gap, I felt sick.

Ultimately, my grandfather took me to the nearest doctor, some twenty minutes away, while my grandmother stayed at the house, in case my parents, who were in Pittsburgh for a wedding, should call. He did not, however, take me straight home after I had gotten the five stitches. Instead, he stopped off at a bar, "just for a minute," and came back almost an hour later, drunk. In those long minutes I spent stretched out in the back of his car in a parking lot, I suppose I experienced for the first, and last, time the man with whom my mother grew up. I had it easy, though, because drinking no longer made him mean as it once did. Rather, it made his shoulders slump and his face sag. It made his eyes heavy and watery and his voice soft. It made him sedated.

That was only one incident, though. The rest of my experiences with my grandfather are much more pleasant. In fact, I can honestly say that he has never been anything but loving toward me. My mother, even, seems to have made her peace with him. It is as if he had never been anything but the perfect father. As far as my grandmother is concerned, I feel the same way towards her. My mother, however, still has difficulties. It is not a matter of my mother not loving my grandmother but, rather, that my grandmother seems unwilling to allow her to do so. It is as though my grandmother resents my mother for some reason of which I am not aware and, because of this, she seems intent on inflicting pain and guilt in her in subtle, but effective, ways.

"I can never talk to her without coming away feeling bad," my mother tells me. By "bad" she means guilty, for not being able to visit my grandmother more often. Even though my grandparents only live two and a half hours away, visits, either way, are rare, and the telephone conversations as they come to this subject, always end up sounding similar. It begins with my grandmother complaining that my mother never visits. "Maybe you don't even want to see us anymore," she'll say in a fragile voice.

"That's not true, we just can't get away," my mother will respond, her head slumping into her hand. And she is telling the truth. My father works all week and only rarely gets a Saturday off, and to drive up and back in one day on Sunday is hardly worth the couple of hours they would have together. From this dead-end, the conversation quickly moves to the next, which is my grandparents coming to our house. At this, my grandmother puts up a wall of excuses; she would have to get somebody to water her plants, she has a doctor's appointment coming up, or her arthritis is particularly bad. But eventually it works its way down to, "This just isn't a good time." And so they go on in their dialogue, talking straight past each other.

Today I sit and wonder, in fact, if I had just been doing the same thing as my grandmother that afternoon, when I called my mother "Dorothy." I have thought about this a long time but still do no know why I would want to hurt my mother. She can be unpleasant, but she can also be kind, and she can be fragile. I understand this now. She worries often about what she is going to do with the rest of her life. For twenty-four years she has been a mother, but now my brother and I are both adults, ready to move out and away. "That is my life," she says, "that is who I am." She worries that we somehow resent her and that we will leave and not come back. "Will you visit me?" she asks. Yes, I will visit you, Mother.

A Puddle Full of Endings

Joshua Mooney
Spring 1991 – Volume XII

The rain was not heavy; it came down sounding a gentle pit-pat on the black tarp above our heads. The rain was like music, nature's ballad, as the white-haired priest read slowly from the small black Bible in his hands. A sob. I gazed over the shiny blue coffin, which reflected distorted images of myself out into the rain. The rain came down all together, yet each sparkling drop was different, defined from each other; I followed each drop down to a small puddle which formed on the mound of earth. The puddle's shiny surface danced and rippled, as each drop broke the surface, losing its shape, entering obscurity.

Across from me was Paul. Dressed in a black wool trench coat, his eyes hidden behind shaded glasses, I could not follow his gaze. Was he looking at our friend's resting place, at me, or at the rain? I remembered back to when I last had seen him, almost three years before. At times, I had thought that our friendship would last forever, but somehow I had known it wouldn't. Everything ends.

But it is endings which give life its flavor and meaning. What is life, but endings? There are different kinds, and at the funeral I was experiencing two. I was saying farewell to a friend, while greeting another friend I had buried long ago.

When I was young, my father used to take my friend

Paul and I to the Bills' games. To me, there was nothing better than a football game in late fall. The crisp cool air, the aroma of cold beer, the steaming hot dogs, the roasted peanuts in salted shells, and the darkening sky – I loved it all. Every week seemed to be based upon whether the Bills won and to see the giant black scoreboard light up in cold white lights. Nothing could compare to the tension and anticipation which knotted me up and wrenched my insides during a close game. "Down by five, with ten seconds to go! The QB drops back; someone breaks through the line!" I feel my heart lurch in my throat. I see Paul flinch. The high pitched screams of girls ring in my ears. I cry out. "But the QB evades the sack! He scrambles! He fires a fourth down pass!" The ball floats in the air; I can count each cycle of the ball's spin. Not a sound is made. I can't breathe. "It's caught! Touchdown!" The tension explodes inside of me, inside of everyone – we all roar at once.

The bleachers tremble and thunder under the stampede of our feet, which pound the silver metal below us. Paul and I exchange high fives. My father gleefully finishes his beer. We are all overcome with a rush of ecstasy. "What an ending!" someone yells. "What a game!" But next Sunday will be a different game; this finish will not matter. This win will be in the past.

Endings make life. They divide life into slices. Yet once an ending is passed, it becomes intertwined with life's vigor. Like a drop in a puddle, the drop is no longer a drop, but part of the pool. An ending is no longer a single occurrence, but part of life. I remember when Paul and I entered junior high. We were fresh from Dodge Elementary, where we had ruled the school. Now the hallways were like caverns, and the older students looked like giants. We went from "who's who" to "who's that?" Our only comfort in those vast hallways was that our insignificance would eventually end.

Days, months drift by, fading into our past. New faces and new teachers – they all floated by and faded back into obscurity. Like a passing ship, they remained a part of our experience for only a short time before sailing off. Only, we were the ones leaving them behind. And though those bonds have ended, they will always be a part of our lives.

Some endings, of course, are more significant than others and are marked with levels of achievement, such as a high school diploma or a college doctorate. Other endings are small, and often go unnoticed, like the end of a song or a relived memory. Endings, like raindrops, gather and form a puddle or pool which we call life. We are unable to see our lives ending by endings, but if we gaze at them, like gazing in a puddle, we are able to see a reflection of ourselves.

The importance of endings was hammered into us from our youth. In the endings of fairy tales, the prince always finds the beautiful, but unknown, maiden. Every ending in a childhood tale finishes with a tender kiss and a "They lived happily ever after." The story is then complete. Time to move on to a different tale. Other endings are not concluding endings, but merely stepping-stones to a new tale. In trilogies, such as J.R.R. Tolkien's *The Hobbit* and *Lord of the Rings*, there is never a final ending until the last book. Sometimes we experience those endings – the conclusion of a football season or the saying goodbye to a friend. But most of the time, endings seem permanent, though we long for more.

As a child, I had always wondered how Dopey and the other dwarves live after Snow White had left them. "It doesn't matter," Paul once told me. "The story is done – there is nothing more to say."

To help us believe life is happy, children's tales always end on a joyous note. The same is true with movies, and we are adults! Movies with sad endings are not liked by the public and generally are not produced. In *The Natural*, who would have liked it if Roy Hobbes struck out in the end, instead of blasting that towering home run which won the game? In the book, he did strike out. People do not like sad endings in fantasy because there are too many sad endings in reality. Maybe Paul was right. After an ending, that's it. There is nothing more to say, so people want to leave the theater or close that book feeling happy.

Sad endings make the most ripples when they enter our lives; bitter endings linger the longest. A tragic ending in a story can often stir up bitter emotions felt in life. Like in life, people want to correct tragedies in fantasy but are unable because the story is complete. The only way to correct the tragedy is to go on, but the ending makes that impossible, something which cannot be avoided. Trying to delay or prevent an ending is like trying to catch rain. When I was young, I used to try to catch the rain. The water would only slip through my fingers; the tighter my grip, the more the water ran.

I remember it was a cool but humid night. Paul and I were sitting on lawn chairs on the lush fourth fairway of the golf course behind my house. The grass was wet, and the earth was soft from the rain that fell earlier that day. I could still smell the rain. The grass clippings stuck to my naked feet and gathered in between my toes. Far off in the trees, which formed a large, ominous black mass in the green moonlit plain, I could hear the breeze rustle through the leaves. Below, the crickets chirped their ballad. It was late August, and we were watching the lunar eclipse. More importantly, we were saying goodbye. Paul would leave for college the next day. We knew our closeness would fade; it had already begun to. We told each other we would write, though we knew we wouldn't. We sat on those chairs, talking of our future, and sipping our beers, as the dark sky quietly swallowed the bright white orb. The area around us grew dark. When we finally parted, there were no tears, no grand farewells. "See ya," was all he said. There was nothing else to say. I grinned and stumbled over my feet. As I walked away, feeling lightheaded and having a lump in my throat, I couldn't help but feel alone.

Unconsciously, I must have realized from the start that our friendship would eventually end. After all, endings are the way in which we live our lives. Happy and sad, our lives would be nothing without them.

Over a year later, I received a letter from Paul. It said he wouldn't be coming home that summer; he had landed a job in Boston and was going to spend the break at his sister's place. It said also that his parents were leaving Buffalo, moving down south to warmer weather. After I set that letter down, I wept. I didn't think I would ever see him again.

The rain slowed outside to a drizzle, and I lifted my gaze from the rippling puddle. I looked at Paul. There at the funeral was the first time I had seen him since that summer night so long ago. I placed my hand on the cold steel coffin and choked out a goodbye. I then reached over and grasped Paul's hand, and said hello.

Dairy Product Princesses

Melissa Grossman
Spring 1991 – Volume XII

Occasionally, I am bothered by insomnia. It is the flagging energy the next day that makes it unpleasant for me, not the fact that I'm caught by the stillness of the night pouring through the shadows of the window bars above my bed. For it is at such times that my mind is fervently alive, reflective and inquisitive, thinking and rationalizing, and positive that I'm finally finding the missing mate to socks lost long ago, even though they sometimes return rumpled and damp.

Woven at the base of much of this flood of recollection is a subconscious sensitivity to the places to which they're attached. This happened when we lived here…and that happened when we were here…this happened after we left…maybe we should have never left…or rather it was for the best we moved on…

To keep sane, it's necessary to realize that I can think too much, attribute too much, reconstruct a place too rigidly. Even more pressing fatigue is often the result, and I'm apt to regard such an "all-nighter" as a waste of precious sleep time, but this negative attitude is more a reaction to overexposure to the mind's horde of sensitivities and collections of home movies, not a wish to prohibit future delvings.

The places I naturally drift towards exploring can only receive a timid guess as to why they stick to me so fundamentally. But I have discovered it is the places that have maternal associations, that is, ghosts of my mother, that have shaped me. Oddly, I have not ever really experienced these places that are a piece of her legacy. It isn't the locations she's passed on, but intense anger and frustration and sorrow, filtering down from her in secondary forms.

As a child I would sneak into my parent's bedroom and pry into my mother's dresser. In no way were the results of such a risk guilty of teasing me to the degree of fascination I insisted upon them. What finds I considered significant, and worth writing about in a pocket-sized notebook with invisible ink, were materials, trappings, objects, not treasures – a watch pendant, a filigree pin, black leather gloves lined with rabbit fur, a peau de soie evening bag lined with shell pink silk, embroidered celery-colored silk jewelry cases, a mink collar from the first coat my father bought her wrapped in tissue paper, and an orange plastic case of old make-up. The things that I've come to understand as valuable, I cannot feel their weight. Opaque and sometimes seemingly bland are the stories I might have heard, but not the sentiment – the white cotton gloves she wore as flower girl at an alcoholic uncle's wedding, a black and white photo of her dressed in white confirmation finery, strands of hair in an envelope, a prayer written in Polish on parchment, a ribbon from her high school uniform, a hand-sized stuffed puppy. They were some of the contents of a forbidden dresser in a forbidden room, and although I'm sure my mother never feared we would become familiar with why she kept them, it was threatening enough to her for us to see or to touch them. The danger and the defiance of the exploit was far too attractive to resist, with the threat of the wooden spoon across my behind adding to the adventure. It never occurred to me how seriously I was violating an impermeable barrier my mother had passionately built against her past.

Other insomniac nights when I'm dragging around the family room I pause by her "library" of romance novels. I read the predictable synopses on the back and make note of cleavage accompanying the color of hair (black and red hair seem to have more), despising their existence in the house and despising my weakness of even picking them up to poke fun. I consider the cheapening agent on an otherwise comfortable room. Every night my mother reads one, sprawled on the same spot on the couch. Every night. Those shelves have witnessed years of new romance novels eventually harvested for "newer" ones. I cannot read in that room, for I believe it to be tainted. Instead I have been squeezed out by hack writers onto the less comfortable living room furniture to read of worlds beyond ballrooms and bosomy governesses forced to be vamps. At three in the morning, when my bed is disheveled and uncomfortable, the cable is out, the pantry is bare, and I've no recourse but to read myself to sleep, the situation is expressly annoying.

Somewhere, somehow, I made a strange alliance of romance novels with ruralism. A consequent myopia has developed within me concerning the Lancaster era of my early childhood. It's a myopia, not unlike the one E.M. Forster exhibits sometimes in Dr. McGuiness: *Pharos and Pharillon* towards Alexandrians. There is the tendency to brand people of an area with a generalization, lumping them together for the same fault. My mistake is in pinning non-cosmopolitans as hicks. Forster's error was to suspect every Alexandrian to have the screaming, frenetic cotton merchant within him.

These generalizations aren't reason or cause of dislike. Rather it's often the contrary that occurs. Forster found a lover and a friend in an Alexandrian, and I have some colorful, unjaded memories. As a child I adored living among a patchwork quilt of farms and fields, Mennonites and Amish, housing developments, and towns in need of renewal. The basement of the mall used to be a genuine farmer's market. Rusticity covers that part of Pennsylvania like a dewy film through which one can choose to break through or sink into the moistness. Movement isn't out of the question, but it isn't a place to be temporary. Spring promised girls--in lavender and wedgewood blue chiffon dresses--that would grace the mall square like gift shop figurines for the Miss Pennsylvania Dairy Princess beauty contest. White gloves up to their elbows, tiaras of silver sparkle paper, white satin sashes identifying their home county in black letters, robin's egg blue eyeshadow, and stiffly sprayed hair rolled and teased; carrying trays of butter spread on Triscuits, or wedges of cheese, or Communion-sized cups of milk. I shy around them, nervous that they would ignore a request from an eight year old, face sticky with orange soda and soft ice cream and bemused by the pastel tawdriness and pageantry out of my reach, satisfied by the thin colors and the proudly worn sashes. The irony is that contest prizes were scholarship money and PR exposure. These girls, contestants of a Miss Agriculture something or other, were stretching for somewhere and something else.

I myself, often search for the perfect, unbruised fruit when reaching back to places. Julys meant that my mother would haul her kicking, screaming, and howling children to pick raspberries for a morning. We detested the labor forced upon us for a few hours in shadeless acres of fuchsia and rich green berry fields. Mother would insist we stay until we picked about thirty pounds of berries she'd create into the jelly we adored on muffins and pancakes. We moaned about the mosquitoes, the nasties swarming in the soil, the lack of soda to drink, the overabundance of lemonade, the prickers that stained our arms and legs with red, smarting welts, and the way we had better things to do, such as building forts and tetherball. The truth is we were having a marvelous time, throwing worms at each other, perfecting our echoes across the fields, and taking exaggerated breaks to ask questions of the black bearded Amish man who took our half-empty berry baskets and poured them into a splintery wooden crate with Stolzfus stamped on the side for the final weighing. Lunch would mean stopping at the McDonald's drive thru on the way home. Our bellies, already bloated with berries, were tortured again with burgers, fries, and soda. Sunburnt and exhausted, we lolled in front of the TV until dinner, while mother sorted berries.

I don't believe it's possible to erase completely the perimeters places have marked around me. I can turn my back on them, yet with one finger fixed on a boundary. I have a fondness for Lancaster, for its backwoods, its homespun web, but that remains only as long as it keeps its footing in the distance, for it is the distance that makes it dear. Perhaps that is why my mother keeps the ribbon from her uniform even though she detested the school and the stuffed dog that was her only present one slim Christmas when my grandfather had been laid off at the Ford plant. She has pressed a certain amount of space between her and these sorrows that happened when she was growing up in Cleveland. Although she keeps her back, rather than a thumb, stiff against the border, it is because that allows her to say she was able to go beyond them, without losing the humanity they molded at the base, at her feet.

Dust of the Ground

Kirsten Sundell
Spring 1992 – Volume XIII

The results of a conception and its completion are almost never the same. An artist, of whatever method, begins, as motivation, with an image of the perfect painting or poem, and sets about to put it down on paper, canvas, clay or stone. From there, the act of creating is a sort of transfusion, a process of transferring one's consciousness through the hands into a pliable and receptive medium, an act that requires balance and understanding between hands, eyes, and brain.

The potter is not often considered a fine artist, but watching a wide-mouthed and perfectly symmetrical bowl arise out of a deftly handled lump of wet grey clay makes molding earth seem no less artistic or creative than dabbling in a box of pigments. The potter before me is making a set of utilitarian bowls and vases, all in a wide, sweeping style. His hands are white and cracked like a sere desert, thoroughly saturated with clay. He slaps down an angular slab of grey-brown earth, briefly pounds it into a rounded mass, and pumps the treadle of his potter's wheel. "Call me a ceramicist if you think it sounds better," he laughs, flicking me with muddy water and applying now wet and darkened fingers to the spinning earth beneath him. The clay responds to his touch, edges spring up where there was only a shapeless lump, the mass starts to resemble a bowl. The potter talks thoughtfully, slightly distracted, as the earth spins beneath his hands, describes how he got started making pottery, what he tries to create in his work.

"It has to be functional," he says, "but the shapes come from inside, really, I just see them in my head and try to get them into the clay." His fingers leave thread-like trails as he shapes and balances; he breathes quietly, scrutinizing the depth of the bowl, the thickness of its gracefully sweeping rim, giving the treadle an occasional push. He gives the bowl a delicate base, small in circumference, that expands out into a beautiful and arching space, almost perfectly round. The wheel slows, then stops, he steps back and studies his handiwork, a smile forming under his mud-spattered moustache. "Not quite what I had envisioned," he comments, "but I like it." He slices the bowl from the wheel with a thin wire, while I sit amongst the greenware on the studio shelves, pursuing his remark.

As an artist, I have contemplated the disparity between the visualized goal and the finished product, the process by which an original idea is conceived into form. I begin with a vague idea, a flash of color or graceful line seen with brief clarity in idle moments or while I sleep. Conveying it the way my mind sees it is sometimes frustrating, the task complicated by new ideas, distractions, the obscurement of time making recollection hazy at best. Standing in front of a canvas of bright flowers, brush poised in hand and ready to apply the perfect hue, I may be struck by a sudden insight or doubt, a fresh idea leading me to alter the direction in which I take the work, or to scrap the piece entirely. The distraction of daily occurrences and the pressures of other responsibilities pull me away from a work in progress, and when I return I often lose sight of what I was attempting to achieve. Being only a fledgling artist, I do not have the ability of the experienced craftsman to accept the disparity between what I envision and what my mind and hands create, to accept as equally beautiful the seemingly imperfect work. Putting it on paper or canvas, or shaping it in the wire foundation of a sculpture, I am dependent on what my eyes and mind conceive as good, on a dim remembrance of a perfect form or color. At some point, I see that I am finished, that there is nothing left to be done with the work, that further molding or application of paints would make the work seem forced, false to its own nature. The potter appreciated the divergent beauty of what his hands had molded, pleased by the bowl he sliced from his wheel, but I am usually disappointed by my inability to completely translate my ideas into form. In creating, the artist is reliant on the accuracy of memory, the skill of his hands, an innate and intuitive sense of balance. The finished work resembles the envisioned only if the artist can accept and appreciate the variation between goal and realization, and only then can he release his visions in the form of great or useful art.

A week has passed, and I have returned to the studio to watch the newly-fired bowl receive a glaze. It has come out of the enormous Swedish kiln a light brownish pink, the color of the pueblos. Holding it up to the light, the potter studies its curves, deciding on the colors and textures of glaze that he will apply, choosing an appropriate finish. As I sit making a pinch pot out of a spare lump of clay, he shakes and mixes great plastic jars filled with liquids and sediments, talking about how he chooses the colors he uses, where his designs come from. "I like abstract designs, big swatches of rich color, transparent hues, a heavy gloss and sheen to the finished product," he says, stroking a glaze laden brush quickly over the surface of the bowl; "Sometimes I just try to show things I see in my dreams. Isn't that strange?" Watching the opaque and sandy solutions sink into the fired clay, I don't think so. I watch carefully, studying the lines and expressions that cross his face as he works. He bites his lip, seems almost absent-minded as he spatters and swathes the surface of the bowl. "It's done," he says, and I snap back from my contemplation, eye the bowl that he holds out before me. The colors are washed out, pale and rather lifeless, like all glazes before they are fired. "I've chosen a lot of blacks and blues," he says, "and a very lustrous leaded glaze. You couldn't eat out of it, but it will make a lovely ornament or flower bowl." I thank him for letting me watch him work. He wishes me luck with my own creative endeavors. I cannot come back to see him again soon. As I leave the plain brick studio, I think again about the creation of art, about the constantly different results that come out of a creative inception. My own work comes out unlike the way I conceive it, possessing a different character from the brief vision upon which it is based.

Like musical variations on a single simple theme, each work captures only a portion of the central idea, elaborating and expanding it into new dimensions. The artist, like the composer, must embrace what he has created, acquiesce to his finished work whether it has captured completely the form or musical concept he has envisioned or not. The true artist welcomes variation in his works, celebrates the singular beauty and worthiness of every piece he creates.

Weeks later, I arrive home to find a low box on my doorstep, addressed to me. Pushing aside the shredded paper, I see the bowl, gleaming black and blue like a great winking eye. Lifting it carefully, I see words inscribed on the smoothly hollowed base. "For K," it reads. "Good luck." I carry it inside, clear off the table, opening the windows so that I can see it in the light of the sun. It is gorgeous, iridescent in the light, with dreamlike waves of deep blues and black covering its surface, speckles of an emerald green rising out of the blue base like evening stars. I am spellbound by its simple elegance, by the depth and clarity of color, by the confidence and creative intuition the potter had in foreseeing his finished work. Guided only by a half-seen vision, his hands and eyes shape what he knows to be good, balanced, harmonious. Conceived in the mind, the creative idea takes life in the hands of an artist; given proper care and gentle encouragement, it can be born into a glorious sculpture, a vibrant painting, a rhythmic poem, a shining bowl waiting to hold lilies and water.

Natchez

Sarah Moran
Spring 1992 – Volume XIII

Every Easter my family traveled to Natchez, Mississippi to spend our annual spring vacation with my grandparents. We always looked forward to this trip. Everything about Natchez was beautiful this time of year, with looming, beautifully green trees draped in Spanish moss, dogwoods in full bloom, and the sweet smells of jasmine, crape myrtle, and sweet olives lingering in the warm air. I loved it there. In Natchez, the beginnings of spring mark the week of the historic Pilgrimage, where tours of the beautifully kept mansions go on throughout the town. While tourists came from allover the country to experience history, for us children in my family, it only meant dressing up in hoop skirts and pantalets, sitting on the front porch welcoming visitors, and celebrating with tea parties on the back terrace.

Since the time spent in Natchez always fell during the Pilgrimage, we were always able to attend the annual pageant held in City Hall. My grandparents took us children out for quite a magical night, staying up late watching the different dances and skits take place in the huge auditorium. The pageant remains vivid in my memory. I remember watching the children dancing around the Maypole, the girls in their brightly colored dresses and hoop skirts, the boys dressed in knickers, and colorful streamers looping through the air to the music of the orchestra. I watched as Natchez residents depicted the marriage of Jefferson Davis to Varina Howell, the landing of the riverboat, and the Audubon, where the dancing master instructed the students, with the girls dressed as boys in velvet suits and other girls in tutus. Every time the polka started up, I was so excited when the dancers came up into the audience looking for partners.

I can still hear the black singers, dressed with long skirts and aprons and kerchiefs tied around their heads, singing spirituals and "Dixie." My mother now tells me that the blacks refuse to do that scene anymore. They believed it depicted them in a lowly, degrading manner. The blacks were simply tired of being portrayed in such a menial way. To me, it was just beautiful music. But finally, when the magical night had ended, we walked home, stopping only to buy pralines from the man outside City Hall.

The pageant, as well as many other memories from my childhood, revolve around our Easter trips every year. Gradually the temperature warmed as we left the cold behind in New Jersey and neared our destination. The weather always seemed perfect in Mississippi. We watched the trees transform along the road from dingy and bare to full and green. With me and my three siblings cooped up in the back seat of our station wagon, we certainly never let my parents forget we were still back there, anxiously awaiting our arrival. The twenty-three grueling hours in the car required as much entertainment as we could possibly fit into a five-by-four-foot car space, including walkmans, unopened books, word puzzles and many snacks. Entertaining ourselves with as many contests as we could possibly have in the car, including counting all the different license plates traveling to Natchez for the Pilgrimage, only momentarily occupied us; therefore, for my family to actually get in the car and travel for so long, the trip had to be worthwhile. It was. For me, Natchez represented many things when I was younger. First and foremost, my grandparents were there. Because we only got to see them twice a year, once at Christmas in New Jersey and once during Easter in Mississippi, we were always ecstatic to see each other. They were so special to us. Every Sunday, I remember anticipating the weekly phone call from the South and listening to my mom's Southern accent instantly return as she heard her parents' voices. I could picture my grammy and grampa in their home, each on a different extension, relaying the news to the family, and not without each of the parties talking at once. It was always completely different, though, to finally be down there with them.

Finally we would arrive to see my grammy and grampa waiting by the front window of their beautiful house, just as excited as we were to see each other. I was always especially excited to see my grandmother. I remember believing she was going to be a saint, in this far away, almost heavenly town that seemed another world to me. She had such an impact on me. Often she slipped me candy or a two dollar bill, telling me to just put it in my pocket. I remember climbing into her huge canopy bed where my grandfather had been born to lie next to her with my brother and sisters while she held her rosary and said her morning prayers. Every morning my grammy woke up with a tear in her eyes, yet she didn't seem sad – I thought God had dropped them in there as some kind of symbol of her holiness.

At night we'd climb back up and she'd tell us story after story, usually about three little girls and their little brother and the mischief they would get into. On some days, holding my grandmother's hand, I used to walk down the street with her, past the mansions of Natchez to just a couple blocks down where there were poor, weather-beaten shacks. Here, she would give poor families that she knew through her parish baked goods and casseroles, but I never knew why. I also never understood why my sisters and I were never allowed to walk further than the front sidewalk by ourselves. I never realized there could be any poverty in a place I loved so much.

For us, Natchez meant Easter time – a time for dyeing eggs and later finding them hidden among the boxwood and rose bushes in the backyard. It meant staying in our Easter dresses long enough to have our pictures taken in the crape myrtle tree. Here my parents taught us the names of different trees and bushes, from the gardenias to the dogwoods, which were my favorite. Here my grandparents' colored gardener Abe planted each of the girls a different little tree. He planted Jennifer a flowering cherry, Amy a flowering pear, and me a white dogwood. My grammy would bring out refreshments, and we would all sit with Abe on the terrace while he took a break from the hot sun and told us stories about when he was a boy.

In Natchez, I grew accustomed to the thick, friendly southern accents that I always wanted to have. These lifelong friends of Mom's family brought over cakes, lemon squares and dozens of more desserts in welcoming the relatives from the North. The overall beauty of the people and the place will always remain with me. But recently some things have really changed my outlook on Natchez.

With the death of both my grandparents, I see Natchez in a new light, and it is amazing to me how much a person's presence can change your outlook on things. Of course, the physical things have changed. Now all the flowers that were kept so nicely in my grandparents' backyard have wilted. The old house that I loved in a town that was so incredibly special to me suddenly changed. For me, the picture transformed from white to black, just as life perishes into death.

When my family learned of my grandparents' deaths, the journey down South was no longer fun, but treacherous. It was wintertime. No flowers were in bloom, and the trees Abe had planted looked lonely and dead. Abe was unemployed. The whole atmosphere seemed dark and dingy; the days, rainy and cold. The life was sucked out of Natchez as we were left with a chilled, unwelcoming air. The house was desolate and quiet, forcing me to look around at what Natchez had to offer now.

I thought back to the Pilgrimage, one of my favorite things about Natchez throughout my childhood. I thought about all the people it draws in annually, and all of the money these people are making from the tourists. But, on the tours, the horsedrawn carriages of sightseers never venture into certain sections of Natchez. For the citizens of Natchez, it meant only showing all of the beautiful, presentable parts to the tourists and omitting the impoverished and still segregated black areas. What I had thought to be a wonderful pageant represented a lot of strife and tension between the black and white population. When we had stopped to buy pralines from the old black man outside City Hall, I didn't realize that that man did not have a home, and he'd been selling candy there for years.

Now I see Natchez as a completely different place, a town that seems set back in time and out of touch with reality. When my grandparents' maid Annabelle and gardener Abe, along with some other friends of my grandparents from the black community, came to the viewing and funeral, I saw tears in their eyes, yet they remained to themselves and in the back. It seemed as if they felt they didn't belong there, that they were going to disturb someone, when these people had been dear friends of my grandparents'. This journey of my own has made me aware of a place where an underlying segregation still exists between the blacks and the whites. I finally realized that if I did go past the front sidewalk of my grandparents' home, and beyond the rows of mansions lined up the street for blocks and blocks, eventually the next block over yields shack upon shack for the impoverished black population. I see a place that is coming to economic failure, and it is not only due to the busting of the oil wells, but also due to the unrest between blacks and whites. With the Civil Rights era, the blacks boycotted the stores, causing the economy and employment rate to suffer. I did not see all of this before.

Natchez had once marked springtime and happiness, a sense of carefree youth – life. Now there is just a sadness lingering about, as well as a resentment towards a place that can be so deceiving. It is unfair that people can be sheltered from the realities of life. Not only was I wrong about my perception of the blacks, but the entire community of Natchez, as well as many other cities in the deep South. There is still this subtle or not so subtle segregation taking place, and it took me many trips down South to become aware of what was going on.

I still have good memories of the Natchez I remember – those of my grandparents, Easter, the beauty of spring in Mississippi, and family friends. Unfortunately, however, for me to best preserve the good memories I have, it is probably best that I don't go down there again to experience the realities of racism and poverty. With such a beautiful, heavenly town that was so far away from home, I guess I was in kind of a dream world when I was down there – with opportunities to attend late night events, get dressed up, and have relatives fuss allover the grandchildren. I really needed to go through a pilgrimage of my own to realize that you need to look beyond what's in front of you to learn more about the world, and more about yourself.

On Living and Things Resembling That

Angela Delclos
Spring 1992 – Volume XIII

The red-inked diagnosis on the board next to acute room three says "turning blue." And I wonder what that means. Usually, the description says "fever, 103," or "SARA" (for sexual abuse or assault cases) or "spice" (an AIDS baby) or "sore toe." But I never saw "turning blue" before that day. The nurse says he – call him Joe – is anencephalic; basically born with only a brain stem, capable of basic life functions (sort of). "Sort of" because sometimes he still turns blue, when he cannot get enough oxygen on his own; and he cannot feed himself or bathe himself or even go to the bathroom. For the twelve years since his birth, nurses and his mother have done it all for him. But at least he remains alive. Right?

According to the medical dictionary, anencephaly is "a congenital developmental defect consisting of absence of the vault of the skull, with an exposed, poorly developed, degenerated brain, resulting from the neural tube's failure to close in the cephalic area; the affected infant usually dies within a few days after birth." This affected infant did not die; he is now an affected adolescent – affected but saved from death.

Joe has no cerebral functions; nothing like cognitive thought or emotion happens inside of his mind. He does not tell his mother, "I can't breathe." He just turns blue.

He does not cry because his lungs hurt and his head aches. He turns blue. So that is his descriptive diagnosis on the main board. "Turning blue."

I wonder who decided to try so hard to keep Joe wondrously living; I wonder if they know him now. I wonder if his mother felt eternally grateful, or if she protested. I wonder if she does now. Peeking into the room, I can see her sitting next to her son, grasping his hand – but her face is unreadable, because her back is to me. Joe is lying on his back, but he doesn't look very blue to me, maybe because they have been pumping oxygen into him for awhile; even at home he is occasionally put on a respirator to get his lungs going. He appears fairly normal from where I stand trying not to gape; the sheet covers him, but he is obviously small, thin and pale. He has light brown hair, a nose, two eyes and a mouth. I do not know why this surprises me. But it does. Like the spice babies that come into the Pediatric Emergency Room (termed for affection and for ease "PED's ER" – long "e" in PED).

The first spice child I encountered surprised me; he was having problems with something called his "portacath." The attendant on duty one of my first weeks there luckily knew something about "porta-caths," which are internal portals for the catheter needle. They provide for easier, less painful insertion of needles for IVs and blood samples, and are surgically implanted under the skin. I can remember seeing the bump the porta-cath made on the little boy's chest, as I grasped his arm to brace him for the prick (that this device made easier to bear, because it eventually creates a sort of "needle callous"). He came to the ER so the doctors could take a fluid sample, because the bump was a little inflamed and he was feverish, so they thought the area may have become infected. I suppose this is too complicated to explain in the seven inch space left on this board for diagnosis, so it just says "spice"

– in blue letters because his case is not acute enough for red. When I first heard the doctor explaining the "porta-cath" to the residents and students, it interested me enough to want to watch the short procedure. His mother did not care so the doctor said "yes."

While the necessary paraphernalia (special needles, saline, sample bottles – aerobic and anaerobic) were gathered, I began to wonder why a nine month old baby would need a little portal under his skin. It would make sense in the elderly and infirm, but in one so young it seemed misplaced. Why would he need the numerous IVs and blood tests implied by the presence of the porta-cath? So I looked again at the diagnosis and tried to think of what spice might be an acronym for; although it had appeared on the board before, its meaning remained a mystery. Finally, in answer to my question, the nurse explained, "Oh, that's an AIDS baby." Hence the porta-cath; he had already had several extended hospital stays (with a new one about to be added to the number) and it can be hard, in babies, to get into the small veins, which have an aggravating tendency to roll around when you try to get a grip on them.

Luckily for the baby, his mother was a nurse and knew how to care for him. She held his hand while we took the blood; I wanted to take my gloves off, even though it is procedure to always wear them in the presence of any patient's bodily fluids, to show her that I didn't care and that I knew I wouldn't be contaminated by just holding his bare arm. Or maybe to show the baby somehow that someone besides his mother was not afraid to touch him without wearing latex over their hands. But bare hands are made impossible because of our rules; I sometimes wonder if I would have taken them off even if we did not have the rules and am unreasonably ashamed. Afterward, the doctor threw the needles carefully into the "uncapped only" needle receptacle – uncapped because it is too easy to prick oneself when putting a cap back on after use. The needle collectors count everyone each month and keep a tab of how many capped needles each department has. They can get in trouble for too many caps.

It is still not clear what spice stands for – I mean if it is an acronym or just a disguise word so other patients do not treat AIDS babies like lepers. Enough people that come through these doors are familiar with the word anyway, so that the latter might not be the case. For instance, the very next week, a six year old boy came in with a one hundred and six degree fever (after Tylenol). When I saw that temperature on the board and sucked in my breath, the nurse said that he was a spice baby, born with HIV. He has AIDS now, and it allowed him to spike a fever that was a record high in the PED's ER. This boy's parents are not with him; his foster parents brought him in, but they could not stay because they have too many others at home. So we gave him Tylenol and kept him under watch. He would have to be admitted. By the time his fever finally went down to 'safe' range, he was sitting out with the doctors and nurses, laughing as everyone teased him about the colorful jungle picture on the wall. He laughingly insisted on the wrong names for all the animals, trying to fool us all. I rubbed his arm a little and squeezed his hand while I sat with him for a while. When I went back to help the nursing extender stock rooms, he told me I should be careful because the little boy has scabs all over his body. He was recovering from scabies which exploded out of control due to his weakened immune system.

Touching an open scab could cause transmission (of scabies). Though it could probably have harmed him substantially, for most people scabies is easy to control and cure.

This child was only two degrees away from dying;

he will be about that close to it for the rest of his life-however long that might last. For now he is affected by the AIDS virus, but still saved from death. And his real parents, both HIV positive, remain in jail while he is shuffled from home to hospital to home to hospital.

None of these children had any chance to choose their "quality of life" before birth; they were born into circumstances uncontrollable. The spice children, well, who knows how long they will live; they are a fairly new phenomenon. Joe could live forever, because we saved him from certain death. We are so afraid of children dying that we go to any length to keep them alive, whether they stay in foster homes living from fever to fever, or in their own intensive care home environment living from emergency to emergency. I wonder what they would say if they had a choice, or if they are truly glad that we always so presumptuously saved them all from death. Then again, do we really have any other choice?

Like most ethical problems in medicine, it is much easier to fix the physical problems than to envision the consequences that might arise from our patch and repair jobs. We are so intent on keeping patients alive that it becomes difficult to ever let them go. Joe was saved from death at birth – where could his doctors go from there? They went to huge lengths so that he could live to, and probably through, adolescence, but left him with no imagination, no emotion, no feelings – just a heartbeat and correctably faulty machinery. And once they saved him, they could not kill him – because he is alive; just not alive. Now his family must live the rest of their lives dealing with that, wondering what is left for their son. Is that even as much as the spice babies, born destined to die, but at least capable of awareness? They probably will not live to see the end of their first decade, and doctors cannot do anything about that. We would all like to play

God, ending death and pain. Sometimes, our hands are tied; in trying to untie them we take the risk of making a bad situation worse. By the same token, in not trying, we risk losing the chance of making the situation better.

> I was determined to learn the difference
> between knowledge and foolishness, wis-
> dom and madness. But I found out that
> I might as well be chasing the wind. The
> wiser you are, the more worries you have;
> the more you know the more it hurts.
> – *Ecclesiastes, 1: 17 -18*

Together We Stand: Divided We Fall

Kristen Roberts
Spring 1993 – Volume XIV

> "Lately, I've been in a life like limbo, lookin' out of a smudged up window. We're not sure where our lives are going, friends, it's summer outside but yet we're snowed in."
> – *Arrested Development*
> *"Give a Man a Fish"*

As the country celebrates, or protests, the quincentennial anniversary of Christopher Columbus's discovery of America, it is important for America to keep its problems in perspective and not to lose sight of the real issues. The 1990's seem to be the age of the politically correct. As we enter the 21st century, we are all aware that it will not be long before the majority of our country will be non-white. Perhaps this is what has given rise to the politically correct education philosophy of multiculturalism. Americans have jumped on the bandwagon of the multiculturally minded, the politically correct.

What is multicultural education? Multicultural education is putting little African-American and Asian-American faces on the school bulletin boards instead of just Caucasian ones. It is making an extra special effort to find books about girls named Lakeisha and Hey Yong.

Multicultural education is teaching that Columbus is not a hero but a villain. Multicultural education attempts to include all ethnic groups and races and to present lessons from their view points. The philosophy behind multiculturalism is correct and fair and should have been institutionalized into our American lifestyle and school curriculum long ago. It causes us to re-examine our beliefs and our view of history and the world around us. Many educators believe that multicultural education will instill self-esteem in students and foster respect for different lifestyles and choices. They also believe this surge of self-esteem will push previously unsuccessful students to work harder in school and thus place in the work force. But will it really do all that?

The increasing diversity of our country, and the problems of dealing with it, have led America towards adopting the philosophy of multicultural education. However, multicultural education alone will not solve our problems. It is merely a drop in the bucket. Once multicultural education has been implemented it may look as though something significant has changed, but little will. America loves "quick fixes," or what appear to be quick fixes, to long term problems. I fear that America will adopt multicultural education as the panacea to a myriad of national problems, such as racial and economic stratification.

If implemented alone, multicultural education will serve merely as cosmetic surgery, making America look happy and united on the outside while corruption and inequality rot away its infrastructure. Smiling faces of every nationality will hang on the elementary school bulletin boards greeting one as he or she enters the building and talk of Native American heritage and the philosophies of Marcus Garvey, an African-American forerunner of the "back to Africa" movement, will fill the high school hallways. However, many children, predominantly those of the lower class and minorities, will still be educated in overcrowded classrooms in decrepit buildings. Urban students will still test nationally behind other students because of the lack of money allocated to early intervention and childhood development programs. Education moneys will still be distributed on the basis of property tax, meaning the average urban youth will receive a $5,000 education while a suburban child receives twice that amount. College admissions will still base acceptance on the SATs which have proven to be discriminatory towards minorities and the bilingual and students of a lower socioeconomic status.

These are the true problems, the real issues. They are what is holding back certain communities. Multicultural education may assure equal cultural content in the curriculum, but it does not assure the much needed equal education. This can only be achieved through monetary means. Supporters of multicultural education argue that it will foster respect and increase tolerance towards social differences among America's youth, thus relieving racial tensions and reducing prejudice. They also argue that multicultural education will heighten the interest level of minority "at risk" students, thus encouraging them to stay in school, graduate higher in their classes and ultimately increase the rate of minorities going on to higher education. The supporters believe that ultimately this would enable minorities to compete in the work force as equals. However, these are extremely high expectations. It is silly to think that the one step of implementing multicultural education will obliterate the myriad educational inequities caused by a conglomeration of serious causes.

Although the philosophy behind multiculturalism is commendable, flaws still remain in the plan itself. Yes, it is important to have an understanding of one's own culture and others', but it is also important to remember that one is American first. I am not advocating the "melting pot" philosophy because I believe that it is our differences that make America so great and colorful and creative. I advocate, rather, the "salad bowl" philosophy described in Frances FitzGerald's essay, *America Revised*... a little bit of everything you have in the house that tastes good together. Marianna de Marco Torgovnick is a fine example of a well-adjusted citizen. She writes in *On Being White, Female, and Born in Bensonhurst*: "I'm still, deep down, Italian-American Bensonhurst, though by this time I'm a lot of other things as well." She warns us not to allow ourselves to take our differences to such an extreme that we begin to feel that we have little in common. It is important to appreciate our differences. It is equally important to stress our similarities. America is a family and just like any family we have more in common than not. As Americans, we have more in common with Americans of another ethnic group than we do with our own ancestral counterparts.

Multicultural education, similar to our present philosophy concerning the education of history, does not acknowledge that all people are human and have flaws. In history books people are either good or bad, heroes or villains. Multicultural education does not attempt to study issues from multiple perspectives. Previously, history was studied predominantly from the viewpoint of the winner, and now it is studied predominantly from the viewpoint of the underdog. At one time, Christopher Columbus was viewed as a hero; today he is beginning to be viewed as a criminal. "Captain John Smith, Daniel Boone, and Wild Bill Hickock – the great self-promoters of history – have all but disappeared, taking with them a good deal of the romance of the American frontier. General Custer had given way to Chief Crazy Horse,

General Eisenhower no longer liberated Europe single-handedly," wrote FitzGerald in *America Revised*. Where we once stood in the shoes of the winner, we now stand in the shoes of the victim. Neither are accurate evaluations. Neither form of education attempts to teach students to analyze the issues in the context of history.

There is a great number of problems incorporated in multicultural education if it is not administered nation-wide. In order to develop respect and increase tolerance of different lifestyles as a nation, multicultural education would need to be introduced in all public schools, not just the predominantly minority institutions. Presently, the minority populations are pushing for multicultural education in their school systems, but few people are pushing for it nationwide. We must learn, as a nation, to appreciate and tolerate differences. Everyone must learn of the great contributions made by each ethnic group, not just students in a classroom predominantly of a specific background. Only through nationwide implementation of multicultural education will we learn to respect each other as well as ourselves.

Another complication of multicultural education, if not standardized as a curriculum requirement nationwide, is that the schools that adopt the multicultural philoso-phy, predominantly the urban schools, will cover new and different materials. We, as a nation, must accept the new curriculum as a legitimate and equally adequate perspec-tive of education. Unfortunately, society is often reluctant to change. Uninformed citizens might criticize the new curriculum as being "watered-down" simply because it is not what they were taught in school. This narrow per-spective and unwillingness to accept change would hold our nation's progress back. It is especially vital that colleg-es and employers view the new curriculum as important and relevant since they are the institutions that provide the needed opportunities and resources for success in our society. This is likely to happen only if the mentality of our nation accepts and adjusts to the curriculum change and if the policy is adopted on a large scale.

As a society, we must acknowledge the fact that we cannot undo what has already been done. We cannot restore the past or give back time already passed but we can give a future to violated groups. Presently, many minority communities are almost completely dependent on the "white man's" economic system. They sleep in buildings built and owned by white people and shop in stores owned and managed by white people. Many are employed by the white business owners. Because the minority communities are predominantly dependent on Caucasians for their source of income and survival, they are not free. Whenever a particular person or group controls the sustenance technology, and thus the profit made from it, they also control the people dependent on the system. An example of this on the small-scale is the relationship between a board of directors to its employees, and on the larger-scale, the relationship industrialized countries have over nonindustrialized countries. These situations are analogous to the relationship of white communities to minority communities in America. In 1965, the great African-American orator, Malcolm X, stated: "We can never win freedom and justice and equality until we are doing something for ourselves!"

Through the creation of education and job opportunities, we give people the opportunity to decide their own destiny. If we create jobs and prepare the targeted students (lowerclass, minority) with the necessary skills to perform these tasks, then all communities would have an opportunity for advancement. We would see a rise in the economic independence, and thus the disintegration of the economic and social alienation of the African-

American and other minority communities. The pride taken in providing for one's family and improving one's community is much greater than the pride derived from the accomplishments and contributions of ancestors who walked the earth hundreds of years ago. When a person cannot put adequate food on one's table, the farthest thing from one's mind is whether one's great-great-great grandfather was king of Spain or emperor of China.

Education experts argue that multicultural education will foster self-esteem in minority students, and to a small extent, this is probably true. However, nothing fosters self-esteem like equality. Multicultural education is more fair and culturally encompassing than previous philosophies of education; however, it is not the same as an equal education. Inner-city students are not ignorant of their surrounding world. When they visit other schools for sporting events they realize that it is only the ghetto schools where the rain falls through the roof when it rains, where the heater has been piping out a consistent 80 degrees for the past seven years.

These are the true problems, the real issues. This is what is holding back certain communities. Besides being morally correct, remedying these issues will decide the future of America as we know it today. America, as a democracy, is dependent on an equally educated populace. Unequal education creates economic stratification and uninformed voters. This creates a nation with little incentive. It also creates a nation that has lost faith in its government institutions and in itself. We cannot allow our students, America's future, to lose hope before they graduate from high school. More money and attention must be given to education in the future. Our nation must change its "nearsighted" outlook on life and look at the big picture. It is a "pay now or more later" situation. In the long run, it costs much less to teach a child a trade or send him to college than it does to support him on welfare or in jail. As the ancient proverb states: "Give a man a fish and he'll eat for a day; teach a man to fish and he'll eat forever."

Multiculturalism may be the first step towards equal education and a less stratified society; however, it cannot be the last. Like an undressed wound, we have let America's racial and economic problems fester for too long and now our nation has a serious infection. Multicultural education is merely the band aid. We must be sure to clean out and treat the wound. Minorities in America, concerned citizens, beware! Monitor the wound carefully. We must be aware that multiculturalism is no miracle "cure-all." We must not settle for merely multicultural education – "the white man's educational table scraps." Demand what has long been due to us – equality, not only in education, but in every facet of our lives.

A Borderless Land

Allison Kelly
Spring 1993 – Volume XIV

An invisible line separates the human world from the realm of the animal. At times it widens into a chasm, vast and frightening, and the lions and great black bears roam on the other side in some far off savage and natural country. Other times the line is thin but sharply defined, when one stares into the large brown eyes of a monkey or the intelligent, alert eyes of a wolf, restless in their zoo cages, behind the rough edges of humanity. And sometimes the line is so narrow and shaky its presence can hardly be felt; one feels only the sloppy kisses of the puppy or the soft, vibrating body of the purring cat. Through their pets, people almost cross that strong, transparent barrier. But the obstacles won't go away; man won't let them go away. Although scientifically classified as animals, humans label themselves superior and automatically and unconsciously reinforce the line. We will never be able to cross over...

It was dark. A fold of black velvet covered the landscape. A chorus of crickets, its monotonous song like the slow, steady heartbeat of the stillness, was in harmony with the peaceful night. Clouds stretched across the sky. Every now and then, the moon peaked through and cast aglow, like the soft spill of light from an open doorway, here and there on the freshly mown grass. A slight breeze sent a whisper through the trees as they leaned towards each other as though eager for gossip. A car horn sounded in the distance, its discordant note of impatience intruding on the quiet hour. A shadow moved out from the ebony backdrop and shuffled across the ground – a raccoon on his nocturnal rounds.

The scraping of the screen being raised earned the flick of an ear, but the murmurings of a human voice did not disturb the evening's observer. After a minute, the window came down with a bang and the curtains were pulled with a swish, shutting out the blackness. The person went back to bed. But the cat stayed on its perch, watching, listening, and sharing with the night.

"Here, pussycat! Would you like some milk? Here, pussy." Pause. "Oh, never mind. Cats are too independent. Look at it! All it's doing is sitting there."

The insect was brown with an oblong body and impressive pincer-shaped feelers attached to its head. It moved slowly, stopping continuously to swivel its sensors and look for anything worth finding. It was only a few inches from the cat's paw but showed no fear as there was no movement from the feline giant. The insect went about its business, unconcerned with the cat's scrutiny. Eventually, it crawled out of sight. The cat contemplated the tiny path the bug had taken through the grass, then curled up and went to sleep.

Sounds. They came in slowly, growing louder as they pushed through the layers of sleep. The cat's ear twitched, but it kept its nose cozily tucked under its paw. The clatter of dishes in the sink caused one eye to open, then the other. The room was dim, the last light of day sneaking across the rug towards the door. One carnivorous yawn. The cat pulled itself into a sitting position and licked its side thoughtfully. People entered the room and sat down in a lot of the cat's favorite sleeping places. Noise blared from the screen across the room and shapes flickered into existence. The cat heard a much more pleasant sound

– the electric can opener's whir. The strong smell of processed fish and chicken wafted into the room. The cat stretched, first the front legs, then the back, oozing the last vestiges of sleep from its body. It jumped down from the sofa and sauntered into the kitchen.

"Well, good evening, sleepyhead. I'm amazed you could drag yourself away, from your day-long nap. You really have the life, you know that? Sleep sixteen hours a day, eat, lie around looking pretty, just waiting to be pet, and you don't even have to work for a living!"

The cat could smell the intruder before it saw him. The odor of challenge, past battles, and dangers preceded the stranger before he turned the corner of the house. Black and evil-looking, the evidence of his fighting history was clear in his muscular body that was so covered with scars he looked like a walking punching bag. He walked slowly, power in his every step, crunching through the layer of fallen leaves, as his head moved from side to side, sniffing out this new territory. If he was aware of his stray status, he did not look as though he cared. Coming within a few feet of the resident cat, he stopped dead and glared. The appointed defender of the property returned the stare and felt its hair stand to attention along its back. A growl started deep in its throat. There was a chill in the air that had nothing to do with the time of year. The vagrant gave a deep rumble of his own. Then the air was split by the eerie sirens of the two cats preparing for their duel...

"Hey, cats!" A person came running outside, scattering the combatants. "Why do you stupid cats have to fight all the time? I swear, I've never seen a more aggressive animal." Pause. "Oh, will you look at that! Okay, who was supposed to clean up the porch? Someone in this family had better get out here NOW or heads will roll!" The screen door slammed shut.

"You don't want to go out. It's snowing." The person finished putting on his boots and was done with the lengthy process of getting ready to go outside. "I know what you'll do. You'll huddle on the porch and look miserable. You just don't appreciate the beauty of nature." Sigh. "But, if you really want to go out, okay. But I'm not letting you in again for awhile. It won't hurt you to get some fresh air." The bundle of knitted and well-padded clothing rose to its feet and opened the door.

The cat sat on the porch and watched the snow fall. Each unique, tiny flake spiralled down from the sky on its own special path. The cold air was sprinkled with the scent of pine, emanating from the tree sprawled on its side in the snow, waiting to be taken in for Christmas. Wrapping its tail around its body, the cat sought its own warmth to combat the sharp, icicle-tinged air. A harsh, scraping sound overpowered the quiet of the falling powder; the sidewalk had almost been cleared, the snow discarded in a blackened pile by the driveway.

"Ah, doesn't the fire feel nice? It makes the room so cozy. Look at the cat. She sits in front of the fire for hours and just stares. What does she see in those flames? Oh, I guess nothing. She's probably half-asleep, basking in the warmth of her own personal sauna."

The cat stared deeply into the flames, watching the reds and yellows writhe in the ecstasy of battle, then fuse together in brilliant color. Hissing and crackling, the wood split apart and melted into ash as the heat reached out and gently massaged the cat's old joints. She closed her eyes. The smell of burning wood was powerful but natural, soothing the senses.

The fireflies switched on, off, on, off like tiny sparks of creation being reborn. The air was moist and heavy. There was no breeze, and the night hung still and silent under a canopy of stars. The air was soaked with the scent of blooming flowers and the fresh fragrance of cut grass. Towering shadows, the trees stretched their twisted arms, silhouetted against the moonlit sky. The sounds of television and the whirring of fans at top speed filtered through the screen window.

The cat was at its usual place on the windowsill, inside this time, watching and seeing each movement, no matter how small, how insignificant in the grand scheme of things. The cat was thinking of nothing and feeling everything.

The television was turned off and a hush fell over the house. A presence drew near behind the cat. A human hand came down to stroke the cat slowly, thoughtfully.

"Why are you always sitting here at this window? What do you see out there?" Pause. "Oh, look at the moon! There's a firefly! Isn't it pretty? You know, you have a really good spot here. Do you mind if I share it with you for a minute?" Together, they watched and became part of the night. And all thoughts, feeling, labels, and lines faded into blackness.

Drawing the Male Figure

Andrea Jayne Sabaliauskas
Spring 1995 – Volume XVI

I drew for three hours. Pencil, charcoal, brick red. My fingers were coated with fine dust, its pigments making the tips look as if I'd stuck them in an electric socket. It was deathly quiet in the Studio despite its high ceiling, which usually acted as an audio magnifying glass, making even the smallest sound echo and bounce off the walls. But until I heard the model's watch beep I scratched away, the sound audible only to me. I paid no attention to heat, which had been cranked up for the model's comfort, nor to flies, natives to the Studio, who buzzed in through the fireplace. This was too new, too sensitive to be interrupted by such trivial matters. I was drawing the nude figure.

And it was not only a nude whom I tried, with the fervent clumsiness of a non-expert, to reproduce on my paper, but a <u>male</u> nude. Our life drawing class had begun with a mere skeleton for the first few weeks, and just as I was getting the hang of sketching fibulas and femurs, the female nude entered, with all the comfort and nonchalance of one whose job it was to daily expose her flesh to an audience armed with pastels. And she did.

For four weeks we drew the female figure. I bragged foolishly to my male friends, "Oh, you wouldn't know it but every Monday night there's a little orgy on the east side of campus." Only Jonathan believed me. "You really sit and draw naked women?" he asked, his voice quiet and laden with tentative acceptance.

I smiled nervously at that. Jonathan was a ladies' man, suave and debonair as a young Bond, James Bond. We'd been friends since freshman year, and a large part of that relationship was being held together by a mutual, unspoken, playful attraction. By far I wasn't the only woman in his life. I had a brief vision of him sneaking up to the Studio around eight or so, up on his toes in the muddy grass to catch a glimpse through the dusty window pane.

"Yeah, I draw naked women. It's life drawing. It's necessary."

I tired of it shortly, though. "When do we get a man, Mrs. Robinson?" I asked my professor jokingly, with a mockingly amorous leer. I thought I had mastered the female. My portfolio was full of thickly-lined, sketchy drawings of standing, sitting, reclining, twisting females. There was no newness to this.

Of course, Jonathan had to know when the male nude arrived. "Have you got him yet? What was it like?"

I squirmed a little. Yeah, we'd got him. It was like walking in on your father by accident when you were young, when he was getting out of the shower. There was the clean soapy smell and the trickle of the leftover shower water falling into the drain and the moist thickness of the air, and these were the only normalities, the only things you could cling to as familiar, as recognizable. In the middle of it all was this soft, fleshy, monochrome figure that you only slightly knew, and having body parts which you never dreamed existed on a human being. I daren't tell Jonathan that this was my first experience.

"Hasn't arrived yet," I lied, "I may need to practice on another model." How brazen this fruitless teasing. Even more brazen – I mentally unclothed him. He was squooshy, as if God had really fashioned him from clay. Was that truly what he looked like? I think I preferred him in T-shirt and jeans. Clothing penned in the flesh, giving it roundness and fluidity. I found THAT attractive. To each her own.

I'm not on the same level as everyone else. I got another C on my homework, a ludicrously stark red curve in the midst of my gray scratchings. The flies danced along the lines of my drawn skull, completing my macabre composition. My heart was seething somewhere within my ribcage. My line was beautiful, crisp, clean. Why the constant rejection? I tried to ignore it as I drew the male figure. Such a splendid blend of curve and angle. No Adonis by any means, but slender, tapering at wrist and waist and ankle. He didn't move despite the flies circling his head, so many small airplanes staking out King Kong. My heart was willing, my hand uncertain. The line was searching. I erased too often, and charcoal dust filled my nostrils. I was unable to do him justice. Why am I majoring in this?

I went tentatively to Jonathan's dorm that weekend. His sweet cologne lingered by the doorway; he was home. He was draped over his bed already, though midnight had barely arrived, and there MIGHT have been a touch of alcohol mixed with the cologne. I felt the need to speak with him even in his unconscious state. "My drawings aren't doing so well," I began awkwardly. "I'm falling behind a little. I guess one day it'll all come together, but I don't think I'm patient enough for that. You know me…"

My face crunched up, my muscles tensed so that my forehead throbbed with a dull pain. Jonathan reached down with one sluggish hand and ran it through my hair. "What happened to my Dreamer?"

I let myself cry. I'm thrown overboard, I couldn't find the lifeline, the water washed over my face. Dare I try to keep up?

I lay down next to him. Almost against my will I faced away from him, a Prufrock afraid to hear the mermaids sing. I breathed in; the coverlets were heavy with his fragrance, and soft to my cheek. I couldn't see him at all. I was like a blind girl waiting, heart pounding, in a seemingly empty room, where a man approaches for good or for evil...

His arm slid around my waist and drew me toward him; I could feel his warmth along my length. My gaze was fixed on his roommate's computer resting, blank and faintly glowing, on the desk beside us. I couldn't turn, however badly I wanted to, however urgent and seductive the whispery voice in my mind became, coaxing me. I laced my hand in his, trying to ignore the knocking of my heart, the shivering of my teeth. If I had my charcoal now, I could shade that hand: a little dark at the knuckles, white at the tops of the fingers, blend a bit where the shade met the light, thin spidery lines where the joints creased the skin. The hand searched mine every so often, but always I held it in check, lest it succeed in finding something.

His voice seemed to come from a small, faraway place, though his lips were so close that they tangled in my hair. "This is...different."

"This is weird." My own voice was wavery. I felt like an astronaut stepping onto the moon for the first time, a little sick and quivery, the chalky space food not sitting well with me at all, light and giddy, floating in an absence of sense, a void of abnormality. When I put my foot down at last, the dust rose up in a sluggish cloud and I wondered why I hadn't decided to go moon-dancing before.

We played hide-and-seek with consciousness until the red, glowing numbers on his alarm clock flicked to six o'clock. His chest ceased its rhythmic rise and fall. The hand danced mischievously along me once more and this time I let it go. I finally had a sense of completion: a few more touches of the pencil and the work would be finished. One cannot always be a perfectionist. Sometimes the Muse touches you sadly upon the shoulder and says, "Look long and hard, put down the stylus, remember, and let go." When he got up and vanished into the bathroom I took my cue and found my own bed again.

My figures became larger, filling the page. I had a mere twenty minutes before the watch let out its shrill beep and the model relaxed. If I fashioned a small part – an arm, a back, a torso – I could cherish the details, round the forms. My lines were swooping, expressive, a bird gone mad. Jonathan hadn't remembered a thing that morning. I was determined to pour my disappointment into the work with some red unblended chalk. Mrs. Robinson was pleased with my improvement. Sometimes an artist has to fall back a little in order to catch up.

Self du Jour

Carlene Bauer
Spring 1995 – Volume XVI

> Boys all think she's living kindness
> Ask a fellow waitress
> – *Tori Amos, "The Waitress"*

> You're talking like a duchess but you're
> still a waitress
> – *Elvis Costello, "Sulky Girl"*

Elaine, our waitress for this evening, comes to our booth at Olga's diner to tell us that they are out of brownies. Just like last time, so this really ticks Carrie off. Carrie is already upset because Elaine is waiting on us – also just like last time. She is slow and "mousy," Carrie says, as if Elaine's limp blonde ponytail and grey Keds will have an effect on our service. I begin to feel for Elaine. I am a customer as well as a waitress, and the kind of waitress that I am is not speedy and dynamic. But I notice the way she has gone about this. All of us have our food except for Carrie, who gave her a hard time when we were here before. I notice that Elaine says "I forgot, we're all out of brownies" slowly, deliberately, reaching across Carrie to set down a plate, then straightening up to look at her. I get the sense that she knew all along that they didn't have any, but hid this information in order to torment my friend. I think that she may not be a bad waitress after all.

She knows that waitressing is about duplicity, dishonesty, and discovering that some truths are not self-evident.

A friend of mine once remarked that she bet I had to "work it" to get tips, alluding to the stereotype of waitress as hooker. The answer, then, being that I worked in a place that prided itself on its "family atmosphere," was no. Although I did know a waitress who, when she worked the late night shift, wore more makeup to get bigger tips from drunk gentlemen customers. Along with the mini-vans and station wagons in the parking lot, there were Cadillacs and beat up compacts, indicative of our other regular patrons – senior citizens and teenagers. This was not the coffee shop of Faulkner's *Light In August*, where the stools were filled with drifters and the waitress "knew the hands of many men." Waitresses don't handle many men, but we juggle many faces, and in that way we are required to work it. We check our selves in at the door, and after that must choose what roles we will perform. Will we be nice to the people who have been demanding all night or not? There is no time to be sexy, between keeping salad dressing out of our hair and picking half-eaten buffalo wings off the floor. At Denny's, getting hit on was kind of an event; it was not often that we were left phone numbers or asked out on dates. There wasn't enough sexuality in the job to work in the solicitous sense, so we had to work facets of shifting in and out of two polar opposites: the angel and the bitch. Neither of which are about attraction, but obedience.

Out of the thirteen servers that worked swing shift, the dinner hour, only two were over 23 – a young mother and our lone waiter. We were all, technically, women, but we saw and referred to ourselves as girls. (My grandmother, at 73, still refers to the women she waitressed with in that way.) Not only were we girls, we had to be nice girls, always on our best behavior while serving our customers. At Denny's, we learned the faintly Judeo-Christian maxim, "Don't fight, make it right." Irritated customers we placated with constant coffee and soda refills, extra attentive service, fake smiles, and we were encouraged to give away free dessert if it would settle them down. We also had to be nice to the cooks, too, even when they screwed up your order and made you feel as if it was your fault. Going behind the cooks' line to ask them sweetly, if they wanted a soda or a shake was part peace offering, part thanks for the extras they would give us and the favors they'd do.

The Victorian notion that women should be seen and not heard – or only heard saying *I'll be right there, no problem* – is embodied today by waitresses. Greta Foff Paules, in her book *Dishing It Out*, likens the waitress to the 19th century domestic. She finds that servile notion manifesting itself in everything from the uniform to the cubicles, comparable to servants' quarters, where waitresses should (but are often too busy to) take their breaks. In the politically correct term "server," which tries to extract the sexism endemic to the work, she is quick to point out its obvious link to the word servant. The deferential bearing of the waitress is similar to the British sensibility of upstairs, downstairs, as she moves from the back of the restaurant to the front, from needed at the table to dismissed. But we often don't get the courtesy afforded by a starched white cap and the genteel address of "Miss." We dissolve into "the short redheaded girl," or "the tall black one." We are the sole reason for the undercooked meal, the butt of a joke to teenagers who leave beer or pennies for tips, someone to whom children bark "More Sprite!"

Disrespect is an occupational hazard and a natural result of the "growing-down" women endure in waitressing. Older customers, meaning well, would tend to adopt us as their own granddaughters. They would chat us up during dinner, ask us where we were going to school. We were sweetie and hon. We were such lovely girls and gave such lovely service. After waiting on them, we would return to take the order of the table with the wriggling toddler and discover that we were "the lady." As in, "Hurry up and tell the lady what you want to eat." All this role-playing can make the waitress feel a little like Alice in Wonderland. She shrinks to girl size, the apron transforming into a pinafore as she becomes the favorite child. Wait a minute or two and she approaches matronhood, tapping her foot as she taps her pencil on the order pad. If the waitress must watch her manners at the table, excused from it she can be the bitch, all grown up and in control.

Carol had made the waitresses on swing shift fear her. She worked the late-night shift and had a habit of coming in a half hour early to make sure our shift had restocked and refilled so that her night would run smoothly. She'd start clanging lids on containers, refrigerator doors. "Whose job was it to fill the salad dressings?" she'd ask, in the tone of a mother who has just come home from work only to find that the laundry isn't done and the dishes are dirty. "Not me," we'd answer, all of us scurrying to far corners of Denny's. In a moment of charitable candor, she told me, "If I didn't do any of this, our shift would get shit on."

She was right. Her bullying worked. If we weren't scared of Carol, we were at least annoyed by her, and did the work to avoid conflict. Unlike other professions, unlike life, waitressing allows women to be demanding. To play the shrew, basically untamed, can get the waitress respect, and can get the work done. If silverware is low, or glasses dirty, she must keep nagging to change that situation. ("Your boyfriend must have it rough," my manager remarked when, for the second time in five minutes, I asked for an order of wheat toast.) But only your coworkers can see your bitchy side; she's to be kept from the customers like Mr. Rochester's mad wife. Assertiveness flaming to outright anger is not allowed, and Carol was the second of two waitresses I knew to have been fired for crossing that line. The other was asked to leave because she told a customer to "fuck off." The lesson was this: you can be all good girl, but only some bitch. All bitch will get you fired.

Yet in a moment of duress, the waitress, in the state of all-bitch, comes as close to reality as the job allows. She throws off all the disrespect, the fragile construct of sweetness and light. Depending on who you talked to, these waitresses' rash acts were either brave or stupid. Brave because she refused to let the perpetual deference rob her of her will. Stupid because she lost her job – and now what is she going to do? The rest of us knew our place and grudgingly stayed there, partly circumscribed by interior design. In the Denny's where I worked, there were no doors closing the kitchen off from the dining room, making all the restaurant a stage. The salad bar, ice cream freezer, pie cabinets and trays were all behind the counters and visible to most of the customers. Waitresses could not storm into the kitchen, doors swinging back and forth in their wake. There was no offstage, so all the sturm and drang of the stiff or the screwed up order was played out for everyone to see – dinner theater on the cheap. Customers were treated to heated cook-waitress or waitress-manager exchanges, and the rest of us would end up doing sideline commentary, whispering the reasons for slammed trays and raised voices.

Even if we did have some curtain to veil our exposed nerves, it still wouldn't have made the job any easier. Ultimately, the physical environment has no impact on the psychological one. There is pressure coming from without and within, and where you crack is of no consequence. What matters it that you try not to. In this job, being two-faced is less of a playground slur and more a desired quality. Keep turning the cheek, keep turning the cheek from stable ("More creamers? Sure!") to not-so ("Those bastards! No tip!") and before long, it might follow, your head would be spinning to beat Linda Blair's exorcist-worthy revolutions. But the waitress must keep her head about her, for the good girl can never let her customers see her sweat, never let them see a tantrum, never move from her caste. She pretends that she doesn't mind printing up separate checks. That she doesn't mind making six banana splits because suddenly some table has decided that they do want dessert, and will not tell them that Friendly's is just a little further up the highway.

This acting gets tiring. Though you could offer the consolation of philosophy and say that which didn't kill us made us stronger. Paules likes that Nietzschean logic; she thinks that a waitress' ability to be tough and servile "attests to her strength of will and power of resistance." But more often than not, the waitress finds that she is not everywoman, it is *not* all in her. Being sweet and apologetic becomes difficult after too many long frantic Saturday nights where the big picture of life is not a baroque study of Cupid and Psyche but more like Picasso's *Guernica*. There is no energy to be nice. In fact, there is a negative correlation between number of years worked on the job and the amount that you care. On day shift at Denny's, the waitresses had hardened eyes, hardened attitudes. I worked that shift only once, and was on the brink of collapse the whole eight hours of continuous full-speed service. None of these women, known only by first names like goddesses, would help me. I got the hint that on this sinking ship, it was every girl for herself, and someone had better pull themselves together.

There was a peculiar logic to what we could feel. We could, for example, hate another waitress. Walking around muttering "I hate that bitch" fits nicely into the tough girl persona. Crying doesn't. It's not allowed. Paradoxically, waitresses' servility is particularly, oppressively female, but in some respects, she has to act like a man. Lips can tremble, eyes can fill up, but she has to bite her lip and steel herself against caring. It's embarrassing to be caught out of character, for it shows too much of an emotional investment in the job. Which is hard not to have when you work for five days a week at nine hour stretches, and perspective becomes inverted to the point that the waitress believes everything hinges on whether the salads get to the table before the meal does.

The only waitress I ever saw cry was Melissa, Mel whose motto was "Oh, screw it." She had served pancakes and eggs on the same plate to a woman who'd asked for them on separate ones. After a series of relays from cook's line to the table, each time with an inedible version, the woman refused to eat and left with her husband, without paying. She sat in the breakroom crying, saying "What did she want me to do? What did she want me to do?" Her hands dangled over the arms of the chair, flopping helplessly as she spoke. "It's just stupid fucking pancakes. It's not my fault he can't cook." She wiped her eyes with the back of her hands. "I don't know why I'm crying," she said. "I must be due for my period."

Melissa's tears were a result of, yet at the same time made up for, the dehumanizing inherent to waitressing. I felt badly for her, but I was relieved. Now she was someone who felt, who had a brother, was somebody's daughter. But she apologized away her self in the same way we talked away our selves during slow hours – nothing but the job, boyfriends, movies or school was alluded to, conversation nothing but an exercise in comparison and contrast, never touching on anything really important. At meetings, or when we came to pick up or checks, dressed in civilian clothing, we'd each eye the other, trying to translate the uniformed self to the t-shirt-and-short one. "You have legs," a dishwasher kidded a waitress, on seeing that she was a real live girl under all that poly-cotton blend. It was as if the body didn't exist.

Who the waitress is after the shift, when the uniform is laying in a grease-and-smoke scented heap on the laundry room floor, is not the point. The point is, can she juggle her tables and time wisely? Even though I was doing well for someone who'd been told not to waitress, the job was overwhelming at times. There was a temptation to stand on the vinyl booths, under the swinging lamps and shout *I have many friends. My parents love me. And, I am an intelligent person. I may have forgotten to punch in your chicken strips as an appetizer, turning your snack into a side dish, but I can write a ten-page paper on Virginia Woolf's use of feminine archetypes.* It was Woolf who wondered, "... who shall measure the heat and violence of a poet's heart when caught and tangled in a woman's body?" But who shall measure the heat and violence of an aspiring writer when trapped in a green uniform and no-slip shoes? Or anybody's heart.

The phrase *going to work* does connote a leaving behind – we left our bodies and our hearts went with them. Woolf knew the answer to her own question. Anything held in long enough would find its way out, and there were moments at the restaurant when heat and violence came to the surface like a bruise, darker in some spots than the other, then fading. Lives touched the perimeters of work in such a way that was soap operatic. Cooks dated managers, waiters now pursued bus boys. It was the long-time workers, though, that divulged carelessly, generously. Sandy had been waitressing since fifteen, and had been on her own since seventeen. Kathy supported one son but couldn't tell you why she married his dad. Beth dated many, many men. These stories, gossiped away to anecdotes in dead hours, were only narratives, seemingly without subtext. At times I felt that I might know what my co-workers felt about their lives; from their talk it was possible to detect what was right or wrong in their cosmic scheme of things. More often than not, though, I could only tell you if they thought O.J. was innocent. It was possible to know everything and nothing at the same time.

It was this sense of missed connections, of an uneven exchange, that kept us college students quiet. No matter how much we wanted to leave Denny's behind, we would take some of it with us when we left, and knowing so much was stealing without replacing. It wasn't our place to get involved – and Denny's wasn't our place to begin with. It was not our station and we were destined elsewhere. (The only way we got through the summer was to keep advent for August, counting one more month, two weeks, three days until we left for school.) Our sympathy was mixed with a kind of silent arrogance. Thank goodness, we thought, we had other places to be on our days off besides Denny's, sitting at the counter draining coffee cups and filling ashtrays.

I discovered, however, that the old assumption of the superiority of higher education over low-paying, low-prestige jobs may be at times false. One of the cooks once told me to stay in college, it was the best thing to do. "They love us college students," said a fellow waitress, "because we show up when we have to. We're responsible." Sure, we came to work on time, but how did that compare to defending unfairly laid-off co-workers at an organizational meeting, or supporting a union? We were punctual, but we lacked moral courage.

It had been raining all night, so badly that the lights had gone out a few times and the roads were being closed off. The parking lot had flooded. Three of our cars were filling with water and had to be moved – but none of us could leave the floor. Emily, however, who had just showed up to pick up her check, volunteered to move them, wading with a nearly healed broken leg out to the lot's knee-deep water. She entered the restaurant, limping slightly, and handed us our keys. She smiled; this was no big deal. We began to fawn over her, repeating "Thanks so much," and "Are you ok?" over and over again. And then Marc: "Oh, Emily, you're a saint."

Emily wasn't even religious, but she did exemplify what Saint Ignatius of Loyola commanded: live your ideals through your work. My Jesuit education had stuffed me with required classes in theology and philosophy so that virtue, justice, and the good were actual, always on the tip of my tongue. At work, though, they went forgotten, like the name of a childhood friend or the author of a half-read book. So what if the people I worked with didn't talk about life with a capital L? The girls who wrote papers on those meaningful capital letter words weren't using them either. There was a duplicity in the esoteric values taught at school. They mattered in a three-o-clock in the morning discussion about suffering and the nature of humanity, but in the context of dirty plates, submerged cars, and layoffs, in the world of the accidental and tangible, they vanished into air. But Emily, or anyone else who bused your table, got your drinks, and took orders for you, put those ephemeral words into the language of the pragmatic.

No one was giving out medals for these displays of courage on the battlefield of the food service sector. Although sometimes, for being good little Denny's workers – staying when we didn't have to so there would be enough waitresses, for example – we would get certificates for free meals, excluding beverage. Still, we all deserved to be canonized. There are separate days that melt into one long string of tense, sunny afternoons where I want to scream because I am the only waitress on the floor, or a manager is cooking because they forgot to schedule a chef. Every day was *Anything Can Happen Day,* and that was terrifying. Denny's in Mount Laurel, New Jersey, gone slouching towards Bethlehem: our center never, ever held.

But we girls, we women, had to make it hold, making up for incompetent managers and co-workers. In order for the place to function, the waitresses had to pick up everybody else's slack. We got our own ice, made our own desserts and salads, hauled drums of ice cream and heavy bus pans, vacuumed, seated customers. We were always lifting, stretching, reaching, running. No talk, no thought, just action. In these moments, the job turned its femininity on its head, contradicting the notion that to be active is male, female passive. Michelle Gubbay, telling her story as a cocktail waitress, characterizes her fellow workers as a "strong, brave little group," sounding more like a chapter out of *Little Women* than *Working Women.*

Omit that "little." It asks for pity. It was the managers, mostly men, that needed sympathy. Paules points out that managers of Denny's-caliber restaurants often find themselves stripped of any authority the white shirt and tie might give them; customers must always be right, and temperamental cooks and servers must be placated. Where I worked we could call in sick, or just not show a few times and still have a job. The only threat our manager posed was to our schedule – it was a safe bet that if we asked for days off, he wouldn't remember. What Paules claims – that it is the waitresses who run the restaurant – is true. Pay no attention to the man on the phone in the back office. Although he is responsible for ordering everything and hiring everyone, it is the waitress' problem when things run out and people don't show up. The manager can run over to another Denny's to borrow a server or more ice cream. He may even pick up and seat tables. But until then, as always, she is on her own.

She is not alone completely, for there is a sisterhood that comes from all this being put upon and rising above. Waitresses know the password: Augustine and Sartre were right. Human beings are a diseased lot and hell is other people. We can spend hours comparing war stories, recounting victory and defeat ("They left me $15. That was after I chased them down in the parking lot."). When we eat out we leave bigger tips and are mostly sympathetic and sometimes more critical customers. And if one waitress comes upon another, there is a knowing glance, an acknowledgement that the woman in front of them is tough. Between them, the secret is out – the notion of the weaker sex is wrong. But waitresses in Louise Kapp Howe's book *Pink Collar Workers* told her that admiration was not easily gotten from those outside the circle. For these women, "Oh, you're a waitress" resounded in the same way "Oh, you're a housewife" does to others. But they didn't really care. They were, one said, "doing good honest work."

Honest work. It is but it isn't. In the 19th century, waitresses were women of ill-repute, close cousins to wayward dance hall girls. The waitress may not be seen as a fallen woman anymore, but she still is not an honest woman. Even though a semblance of truth may be glimpsed in that moment when a fellow waitress offers help, when she ties on her apron she is tied to the pledge of keeping the whole truth out of view from customers and from her co-workers. And what results is an occupation built on contradiction. Use the deference of girls to get tips, but nag the hell out of the people you work with to get what you need. Bask in hard-won sisterhood, but keep a stiff upper lip that would make a marine proud. Tell everyone everything about your life, but obscure the meaning. "Behind," we say, when we are coming through with a tray full of food. It means *I'm behind you, watch your back, clear out, don't move.* It is more, though, than the warning. It is what waitresses are always doing. We clear out of our own way to make room for storefront selves – for whatever self the day, the moment, requires.

The Flight of the Spirit

Celso Barison
Spring 1995 – Volume XVI

When I was a young boy living in Brazil, I built traps to catch birds. Each trap was made of wood and was shaped like the great pyramids of Egypt. The traps were made in the style of a log cabin, with thin pieces of wood overlapping one another. One stick held up the trap on one side, so that only one of its four sides was touching the ground. To keep the pyramid balanced in this position, a second stick would be wedged against the side of the trap on the ground and made to lean against the first stick. It was the second stick that would set off the trap when the bird knocked it over or stepped on it in order to get to the food. This trap was very successful and with it I caught many birds, which I later set free. One time, however, the trap broke the wings of a bird. It was a blue-grey medium sized bird which resembled the common pigeon. Not knowing what to do, I asked my grandmother for help. My grandmother looked at me with her big blue eyes and white bushy hair, wiped her hands on the apron that was always against her frail thin body and told me not to worry; she said that she would keep him in a cage and heal his broken wings. Every day she cleaned his wounds, applied medicine and changed his bandages. This went on for about a month, until one day when I looked into the cage and saw that it was empty. My grandmother told me that he had healed and had flown away, but I was not convinced. Why hadn't she called me when the time came to free the bird? I think that she had secretly put the bird out of its misery. I know that she could not stand to see the battered bird deprived of its freedom in the cage. She had always nagged at my grandfather to let go the many birds that he kept in cages. She knew that the bird would never fly again; and she would say that a bird without wings, without freedom, is no longer a bird.

That is why to this day I can't stand the sight of a bird in a cage, gilded or not. To me this is the ultimate sacrilege; it is the destruction of something both beautiful and free. Although I had felt badly about what I had done, at the time I had not truly realized the fullness of my actions; it took something more.

At the age of fourteen and in the eighth grade, I was forced by my parents to attend CCD with most of the other kids in my class. They didn't take it seriously and neither did I. When the teacher asked us to research a saint for a written report, I wasn't very interested. Most people chose a saint by their first names, John would write about St. John and Paul would of course choose St. Paul. Since St. Celso doesn't exist yet, I chose one of the most famous and most interesting of them.

St. Francis of Assisi began life as the son of a wealthy merchant. He was said to have been a handsome, merry leader of the youth of Assisi. In his early twenties, St. Francis underwent a complete transformation and became famous for his total submission to the vow of poverty. Unlike many of the noble clergymen of the time, he did not distance himself from reality. St. Francis always tried throughout his life to help the lepers and beggars of Italy.

He devoted his life to feeding the poor and preaching the word of God to the world. Thus, one might ask, how is St. Francis different from any other saint? He was not so far aloof from the world that he did not see the beauty in nature and especially in birds. Who hasn't seen a painting of St. Francis with birds? Many paintings depict him holding birds in the palms of his hands or walking down a dirt path in his brown robe enjoying their heavenly music. When I had researched St. Francis, I had read that at the time of his death, hundreds of birds could be seen circling over his house. It isn't too hard to believe when one hears the story of the welcoming of the birds upon the arrival of St. Francis and his closest companions to his most dear wilderness retreat:

> "When they were come nigh to the foot of the very rock of La Verna, it pleased St. Francis to rest a while under the oak tree that stood by the way, and there standeth to this day; and resting beneath it St. Francis began to consider the lay of the place and of the country round about. And lo, while he was thus pondering there came a great multitude of birds from divers parts that, with singing and fluttering of their wings, showed forth great joy and gladness, and surrounded St. Francis, in such wise that some settled on his head, some on his shoulders, and some on his arms, some on his bosom, and some around his feet. His companions, beholding this, marveled greatly, and St. Francis rejoiced in spirit, and spake thus: "I do believe, dear brothers, that it is pleasing to our Lord Jesus Christ that we abide on this solitary mountain, since our sisters and brothers, the birds, show forth such great joy at our coming."

I believe that this story shows the true nature and spirit of the saint. He was so kind and loving of all of God's creatures that it seems proper for the birds to act in this way. St. Bonaventure wrote of St. Francis's meeting with Christ who came down to him from heaven in the form of a man with six wings nailed to a cross. Two of the wings were covering his body, two were raised above his head and the other two were raised as if in flight. Not only are angels almost always, in works of art, depicted with great white wings, but here is Christ himself displaying the wings of a bird.

It seems that we see something of the divine in birds because we have always depicted angels in works of art with wings. The wings are what give the bird his freedom and they are the parts of birds that we see with angels in art. Thus, it is the freedom of the birds that we see as divine. Angels depicted with wings are symbolic of the freedom they possess. When a human being is freed from his or her earthly existence, he or she becomes like the bird and dons new wings. In the old movies, the person who dies and enters heaven is usually seen carrying a large pair of white wings on his or her back. Sometimes, however, when we look at birds, we feel the need to capture this freedom and stifle it. We do this in capturing birds, putting them in cages, by killing them or by injuring them so that flying is not possible. What brings us to do these things is our power-hungry nature. We feel the need to have the power to be able to give or take freedom at will. We are in effect making ourselves into gods in giving ourselves this power. Everyone falls prey to the desire of making oneself godlike at one point or another.

When I was younger, I had somehow managed to get my hands on a BB-gun, as almost every fourteen or fifteen-year-old kid does. The novelty of shooting at tin cans or bottles soon wears thin, and unfortunately you begin to look at moving targets through the cross-hairs. I only shot at a couple of birds before my father brought home a painting which changed me around entirely. He brought home a painting of St. Francis not knowing that he was my patron saint. It was a beautiful painting. St. Francis was seated on a rock and perched in his hands and flying overhead were many brightly colored birds. To me, however, it was not just a painting about St. Francis because when I looked at that painting, I thought his face appeared like mine. St. Francis had dirty-brown curly hair, he had a narrow face and a Roman nose that was an exact duplicate of my own. I was so struck by this painting that on that day I laid the BB-gun in my attic where it lies to this day.

After all of this occurred I felt terrible for what I had done. I felt as if the thread connecting me with God had been cut and the vision had been erased. I had felt this way until my family and I made a trip last December to Italy for my birthday. We took an extensive tour through many of the famous Italian cities such as Rome, Venice and Florence. I remember seeing many of the old Italian churches with their cavernous insides and the many altars where the remains of famous saints lay buried. We visited a church in Padova and I can't remember the church's name, but I remember that outside this church, hundreds of pigeons gathered. There were people scattered throughout the crowd of birds feeding them bread and there was one woman with a pigeon resting on her palm, pecking away at the corn. When I saw her doing this I bought some bread crumbs from the street vendor and knelt down in the square with my palms out in front of me. All of a sudden a grey pigeon flew up and landed on my palm. His claws wrapped around my fingers and his wings stayed outstretched so that he wouldn't lose his balance. He was reminding me to keep my wings out-stretched so that I wouldn't lose my balance.

From Gravity to God

Frederick Strauch
Spring 1996 – Volume XVII

"All science is either physics or stamp collecting," remarked Nobel Prize winner Lord Ernest Rutherford. His views on science illuminate the attitudes of many philosophers, theologians and ordinary thinkers. Like Rutherford, they have only one purpose – to reduce human action and the grandeur of nature to a few mathematical equations and fundamental concepts. The study of nature as a science began with Aristotle's work, *Physics*, which is ironically a very philosophical book. Newton's *Principia Mathematica* presented us a quantitative science, dealing with numbers and equations – nothing more. The three physicists that most people know are Aristotle, Newton and Albert Einstein. Of the three, Einstein has made the most significant contributions to physics. Unfortunately, he is also the most widely misunderstood of the three.

Today, many people regard all of science in the same light. With current developments, who could blame them? Genetic engineering, abortion, euthanasia, behavioral studies, Freudian analysis, "Survival of the fittest," eugenics, nuclear holocaust – the nightmare is now. Science has dehumanized the Earth. Scientists' inventions destroy the environment. Annihilation is a possibility. How could science be good, beautiful, or religious?

In contrast, to popular belief, the revelation of modern physics points in the opposite direction. Science, through these discoveries, shows us a truth and purpose that previously was in the realm of theology. Quantum theory, probably the most important scientific revolution since the scientific method, recognizes man's special place in the universe. Dr. Paul Davies suggest that:

> Unlike all the previous scientific revolutions, which have successively demoted mankind from the centre of creation to the role of mere spectator of the cosmic drama, quantum theory has reinstated the observer at the centre of the stage. Indeed some prominent scientists have even gone so far as to claim that quantum theory has solved the riddle of the mind and its relation to the material world, asserting that the entry of information into the consciousness of the observer is the fundamental step in the establishment of reality. Taken at its extreme, this idea implies that the universe only achieves a concrete existence as a result of this perception – it is created by its own inhabitants! (*Other Worlds*, 13)

This extreme conclusion may seem implausible, but there is another that is even more radical. In contrast to the theories of Aristotle and Newton, the current revelations of modern science make the case for divine creation more acceptable than any other argument since the *Summa Theologica* of Thomas Aquinas. While physics may confuse readers more than Aquinas' Latin, the results are startling. Modern physics shows us that the world and the laws which govern it are not only good and beautiful, but perhaps religious as well.

If Newton's worldview is accurate, there is nothing good, beautiful, or religious in our lives. Our very actions are out of our control. Our choices are irrelevant. Our future is determined by the present, our past seen in the present. The dance of the universe ignores our will. Everything is determined. Newton used mathematical equations to describe reality. His three laws of motion and description of gravity revolutionized science in almost every way. The world was reduced to forces, velocities, and accelerations. What those terms mean is less important than the description of the world they suggest. The Earth, the Sun, and stars follow identical laws. If we could record all the positions and velocities of all the particles in the galaxy, universe, or whatever is out there, one would understand the future and past of all creations. The philosophical interpretation of Newton's law boosted the Enlightenment Movement in Europe. Alexander Pope proclaimed:

> "Nature and Nature's law lay hid in night. God said, Let Newton Be, and all was light."

Newton's world – rational, ordered, without uncertainty – is reflected in Pope's poetry, and in the minds of other eighteenth century thinkers. To them our lives are just the movement of particles through time and space, a mechanical system without faith, hope, or love. If God exists, he is not the universe.

Ironically, the study of the universe began not with science, but with philosophy. The Greek philosophers Plato and Aristotle pioneered many key aspects of physics eighteen centuries before Newton. In their era, Plato was considered an idealist and Aristotle a realist. Actually,

Aristotle cannot be defined as a realist in the modern sense. He focused on the world as he knew it, but like Plato, he never supported his arguments with evidence, other than the proof of "rational analysis." The concepts of form and substance, the allegory of the cave, and many other early Greek philosophical concepts were idealized beliefs introduced by Plato. While Aristotle did not use these symbolic terms to describe the world, he disdained experiments and active observation. Aristotle believed that the natural state of all bodies is rest, not motion – a view we now know to be incorrect. His belief complies with common sense. If we stop pushing the wheelbarrow in the garden, it stops. However, his belief omits any notion of friction or force. Aristotle introduced physics, not as a science, but as a theoretical function of philosophy. He assumed that human reason could deduce the laws of physics from simple principles. This assumption remains common in contemporary science, but today there is an emphasis on experiment as well as theory.

While Aristotle would say that the natural state of bodies is rest, Newton's world followed the law of inertia, which states that a body at rest will stay at rest, and a body in motion will continue to move unless acted upon by an outside force. Aristotle's intuition could explain events on Earth, which are affected by friction and air resistance, but it could not explain the movements of the stars and planets, which appeared to be in constant motion. The Greek astronomer Ptolemy attempted to address this with his declaration that motion on earth is different from the motion of the heavens. In his three laws of motion, Newton offered explanations for all motion, both on the Earth and in the Heavens. Aristotle used theory and philosophical analysis to explain motion on earth, and Newton used mathematical functions and three simple laws to describe motion everywhere.

The tension between Newton and Aristotle disappeared when practically everyone accepted Newton's three laws. During the three centuries between Newton and Einstein, people believed the world was understood, their knowledge was complete, and their will immaterial. Scientists were ready to solve the remaining mysteries of the world: electricity, magnetism, the structure of atomic matter, and the laws that govern them. Philosophically, man had no identity. While Darwin's perspective showed little distinction between man and monkey, the Newtonian mechanical worldview placed man equal to a pile of dirt.

The revolution in modern science leads us to this conclusion: the world is our invention, our creation, and our home. We play a role in it every day. The transformation of impersonal Newtonian mechanism to transcendental hope began this century with one man: Albert Einstein. Everyone knows his equation "$E=Mc^2$." "Everything is relative," a modern philosopher might say. In truth, Einstein's genius extended far beyond a popular aphorism. Beginning in 1905, the patent office clerk in Germany developed two sweeping theories and initiated one that placed humans back into the equation of our world. Many people know the two theories of relativity, Special and General. The most important theory, deals with the realm of the quantum – the microscopic world. Together, these three theories demonstrate that science is not godless, ugly, or impersonal. Science is part of us, and we of it. Our relationship is interdependent.

Relativity has one basic tenet – the world obeys laws. Everything everywhere, here or in the core of the sun, follows the laws of physics. To achieve this synthesis Einstein created a new description of time, space, and matter. Time and space are interrelated, his theories conclude. It only makes sense to think of them as one field of spacetime, with events as the points of reference. Time is not universal – it corresponds to each observer. I have one clock, you have another. If I move in relation to you, our clocks become synchronized. The relationships are not random. Einstein's theories describe how one clock becomes out of sync with another. According to Einstein's *Special Theory of Relativity*, time and space are wound in an intricate web.

The General Theory of Relativity extends Einstein's description of motion into the real world of gravity. Newton's original description of gravity makes little sense – "It is given that the gravitational force between two bodies is proportional to the inverse of the square of the distance." This arcane declaration explained nothing. In one sentence Einstein explained the nature of gravity – gravity is acceleration. While such geometry is purely abstract, its predictions are accurate. Mass, as an instrument of gravity, bends the web of spacetime. An expedition in South America in the 1930's found evidence of such an effect during an eclipse of the sun. Light from distant stars, traveling through spacetime, bent around the sun, changing the apparent positions of those stars. *The General Theory of Relativity* merged gravity with spacetime, thus explaining all of the macroscopic world relative to our observations.

Einstein did not receive his Nobel Prize for either of his two theories. He was awarded the Prize because of his work on the Photoelectric Effect. This effect results from light (photons) colliding with electrons in a metal plate. The ejected electrons create a measurable electric current. However, the effect only makes sense if light comes in discrete packets, termed photons that transfer blocks of energy at a set proportion. The Nobel Committee rewarded Einstein for his logical explanation with the Nobel Prize for Physics. Other physicists used Einstein's explanation to develop a theory that would describe the microscopic world of atoms, electrons, and photons. What they found troubles some, but should inspire all. In the foggy world of these particles, a divine order emerges, based on human will and continual creation.

The quantum world shows how man and measurement directly relate to one another. While Einstein showed that our perspective determines our interpretation of the world, the world still seemed independent of our actions. Spacetime was a frame of reference that could apply to everyone, and Einstein spent his last years trying to unify the laws of physics through pure geometry. He held that human will was too arbitrary, too indeterminate to define all of creation. The universe was still a pre-determined universe. The generation of physicists that came after Einstein used his work to show that we affect the world every day, and our role in creation is as great, if not greater than the role of mathematical laws. Here we find hints of the truly divine nature of our world.

When physicists study small particles, they have to follow new rules of mechanics. New rules are necessary because small particles are difficult to detect. To "see" a small particle and determine its position, one must shine a very focused light onto it. According to Einstein's *Photoelectric Theory*, the more focused the light is, and the more accurately it can determine a particle's position, the more energy the light must have, and the more it will change the particle's motion in an inherently unpredictable way. If the motion of the particle is unknown before the collision, it cannot be determined after the collision. Werner Heisenberg expressed this challenge of particle detection in his *Uncertainty Principle*. In brief, this principle states that one cannot know both the position and movement of a particle without uncertainty. The more one knows about the position, the more uncertain the movement becomes; the more certain the movement, the less we can know of the particle's position. Heisenberg's *Uncertainty Principle* underlies all of quantum theory.

Mathematically, a single function can describe the quantum mechanics of electrons and other subatomic particles. Erwin Schrödinger defined this equation, which is known as a quantum wave function. This wave gives a probable position or velocity of the particle in question. In this way, physics gives a statistical interpretation of subatomic phenomena. However, physics cannot define what will take place when and where. That depends on observation. The world, made up of microscopic particles, depends on our observations and participation. In addition to this fact, the *Uncertainty Principle* indicates that our participation alters the world we observe. The world of Newton is an illusion. We are integral to the workings of nature, not isolated from them. Someone, or something, has given us the power of creation.

Today, there is much debate over the future of physics. Fifty years ago, the accepted version of quantum theory stated that what we can measure is all there is. An underlying order does not exist. Einstein revolted against this view. In response to the *Schrödinger Equation*, he retorted, "God does not play dice!" Now, some physicists believe that there is an underlying order to the universe that can unify the world of quantum mechanics with Einstein's *General Theory of Relativity*, and give a complete description of all physical processes.

Speculation touches the origins of existence, the ultimate fate of the universe, and the possibility of parallel universes. One question resonates in this theoretical and philosophical discussion: why is the universe the way it is? There is no logical reason for our belief in three space and one time dimensions. There could be ten, twelve, or even twenty space dimensions. Is our universe a random one in which intelligent life happens to exist? Or does our existence determine the nature of our universe?

The answer lies hidden in an underdeveloped principle. Physicists call this the *Anthropic Principle*. It suggests that the universe exists in its current form because if it were different – with more dimensions, stronger gravity, weaker electricity, or any other variable – intelligent life cold not evolve and observe it. It hints that the universe is nothing without observers on the inside (who knows what is outside). There is no satisfying evidence for this conjecture, but it begins to explain what we are. Physicists revere the theories of Einstein and Newton for their coherent simplicity. They see beauty in Newton's three laws of motion, which described almost the entire known universe in their time. They regard Einstein's theories as more beautiful, because the concepts are dictated by the theory, not arbitrarily included to support observations. Some physicists see the *Anthropic Principle* as beautiful because it touches on the ultimate question: "Why?" Unfortunately, others see that the principle merely responds, "Because." The world of beauty finds a partner in the beauty of scientific theory; however, the jury is still deliberating.

The most beautiful scientific theory would be the unified theory of nature. Such a theory would describe all the forces, particles, and interactions we could ever imagine. It would show us the movement of creation, and the ultimate fate of the universe. Physicist Michio Kaku discusses this in his book *Hyperspace*:

> "It's been called "the greatest scientific problem of all time." The press has dubbed it the "Holy Grail" of physics, the quest to unite the quantum theory with gravity, thereby creating a Theory of Everything. This is the problem that

has frustrated the finest minds of the twentieth century. Without question, the person who solves this problem will win the Nobel Prize." (Kaku, 136)

Some physicists undertake this quest for prestige; others seek to expand our knowledge, while others hope to add something more to the world through such a theory. The great cosmologist Stephen Hawking felt the thrill of this pursuit when he wrote:

"If we do discover a complete theory, it should in time be understandable in broad principle by everyone, not just a few scientists. Then we shall all, philosophers, scientists, and just ordinary people, be able to take part in the discussion of the question of why it is that we and the universe exist. If we find the answer to that, it would be the ultimate triumph of human reason – for then we would know the mind of God" (Hawking, 175).

Unification would spark a revolution much more powerful than that caused by Newton, Copernicus, or Galileo. It would encompass all of humankind, and perhaps unite us as well. If the world is comprehensible, perhaps there is a purpose to the laws of physics. Physicist Paul Davies comments on this possibility of purpose:

'The laws which enable the universe to come into being spontaneously seem themselves to be the product of exceedingly ingenious design. If physics is the product of design, the universe must have a purpose, and the evidence of modern physics suggests strongly to me that the purpose includes us." (*Superforce*, 243)

It seems somewhat fitting that the study of particles, forces, energies, and motion leads to the conclusion that the universe exists for us, that we affect creation, and that we have an ultimate purpose. Perhaps unification will lead us to God.

If the unification of physics can occur, man's role in the universe must be realized. We are doubly entrapped in the knot, as both observers and participators. We depend on the universe, but it also depends on us. The universe's creation is man's creation. This creation continues when you turn on the television, light a cigarette, look at the sun, or sneeze at the flowers. The only inexplicable things in the universe are the laws that govern it. These laws must have some purpose, plan, or originator. When all of physics is unified, science will end and faith will begin. The role of science in the world does not result in dehumanized devastation, but in realization of the good, the beautiful, and the transcendent. One might say that physicists look for God behind the scenes. If so, the hour might be at hand.

Works cited

Davies, Paul. *Other Worlds*. New York: Simon and Schuster, 1980.

Davies, Paul. *Superforce*. New York: Simon and Schuster, 1984.

Hawking, Stephen. *A Brief History of Time*. New York: Bantam, 1988.

Kaku, Michio. *Hyperspace*, New York: Oxford University Press, 1994.

Digging

Annie Garner
Spring 1996 – Volume XVII

My mother pulls the weeds out of the damp earth in small, neat clumps, the roots exposed, leaving nothing in the ground. Her hands move slowly and mechanically, making sure she uncovers every last bone-colored strand, leaving no remnants to hinder the yellow columbine trying to force its way out of the soil. I look at my own hands, smudged with dirt, grasping the grassy tops of the Bermuda grass which has settled along the border of the flowerbeds as quickly as I can. Stray pieces of grass stand up haphazardly in the smooth blanket of soil as if they are charged with electricity. Their exposure bothers me and I rip at the strips of green, tearing them from their places. The roots stay embedded deep within the soil, and will continue to overrun the flowers. My mother watches me for a moment and wordlessly rises from her crouched position, moving her yellow garden cushion to my section. She smiles and takes over, digging from the buried beginnings of the weeds.

I am like my father. I know that, on the other side of the yard, he will throw bundles of Bermuda grass over his shoulder, attacking it with a fierceness that exceeds even my own. In the end, he will shrug his shoulders, defeated, and watch as my mother bends over him, her hand on his back, fishing for the weed stumps left in the ground.

I watch my mother and I cannot understand why she

doesn't hurry to get things done. The most meticulous tasks are always patiently and deliberately carried out. My father works in bursts of intensity, furiously typing into the computer for hours at a time, refusing to allow for any distractions, moving as quickly as he can. When my mother works she avoids rushing. She used to try to teach me how to sew when I was little and my hands would fidget. I'd stab myself with the needle, and the thread would never stay still enough to go through the tiny loop that it was supposed to. It was more than just the precision required, it was the pace; the fact that sewing forces you to slow down and carry out actions with articulation. Your mind moves faster than your hands.

The bundles of roots sit in the even stacks on the ground, forming uniform rows like Alfalfa sprouts. I look at my hands, finger nails caked with dirt forming brown half-moons. This reminds me of grade school, when one of my friends used to tease me and said I wanted to be "a person who got dirt under their fingernails," because I wanted to be an archeologist. I remember my frustration with digging the weeds, my eagerness to finish, and wonder why I still even consider archeology. I imagine myself, the sun warm on my back, as I bend over a large slab of rock, scratching at the surface with small, deliberate motions, struggling to free a chip of Mycenaean pottery from a crack in the stone. I think of the mental strength necessary for me to control my inclination to pound at the surface, to free it with one powerful smash. Would my hands itch to move in wide arcs, to be released from the small, precise movements as much as they do when I am weeding?

I can envision the next time, the dew forming wet patches on my jeans where I kneel, trying to pull the plants out of the ground like my mother. I will find myself possessed, my hands caught in an unnatural slow-motion sequence which traps my thoughts, slowing them to a similar pace. Already I feel cornered, as if I can't escape, trapped in thoughts that must correspond to action. Edna St. Vincent Millay wrote in *Intention to Escape from Him*: "By digging hard I might deflect that river, my mind, that uncontrollable thing." It is only when I throw the tight bundles over my shoulders as quickly as I can that I feel like I am accomplishing something. And I think it is here that my logic is clouded.

My mother is the real caretaker of the yard, the maintainer of order. My father's garden would be overgrown with weeds, scattered with stumps of grass which would stand up erratically, headless with the beginnings of new sprouts still visible. My mother's hand will finish the same time as her mind, and she will move on. Her measured motion allows her to preserve not only the young lives she tends, but her own knowledge that her job is finished; neither mind nor body will be waiting for the other to catch up.

Watching my mother, I think about the two forms of life waiting to be unearthed, pulled up from the soil – the lost lives that promote a new existence. One dies, the scrawny, wilted leaves uprooted to ensure the growth of other foliage, and the other is reborn, a piece of the past that has been buried for years, now to be illuminated. Somehow the excavation process of the second seems less tedious – it is more of a rescue than the first. A glimpse of the past excites me: the process of discovering ancient lives that merit preservation. But for my mother, it is the new stalks that matter, taking their first breath of a new existence. For my mother, the study of the plant life that she cultivates pulls her closer to the earth, to life.

In a few days, the tips of the Bermuda grass will begin to sprout again, and my mother will return to the ground, using deliberate motions to completely unearth the persistent plant. There is something about the repetitive motion, the interaction with the plants that affects her, making weeding more than just a menial task. She thinks about the amount of sunlight the columbine will need in order to thrive, whether a Peony or an Iris would do better in an adjacent flower bed, and how to ensure that the young lives flourish. Through digging she uncovers the growth of spring. Through her elimination of the runners of roots that plague the soil, she paves the road for Persephone to rise and revitalize the ardent and her world. The tough red clods of clay loosen under her trowel, clinging to the roots, and a transfer of energy occurs – an exchange between the rich, fragrant earth and her. Because she is so involved with the process, it is easy for her to be patient, easy for her to match pace with procedure.

The other day I was talking to friends about what they wanted to do after college. Someone said something about making sure that she earned a large salary, and then someone else said, somewhat accusingly, "It doesn't really matter as long as you are happy." I never consider happiness to be something of permanence, but just like every other emotion, a feeling that passes. Patience, on the other hand, seems to lengthen the amount of time that you are satisfied with something. In the winter, my mother roams the house at the same deliberate pace, satisfied in accomplishing tasks thoroughly and precisely. But there is nothing quite like watching her weed – the process transforms her, resurrects her spirit. The joint finish of mind and body secures her happiness for an extended period of time. Maybe this provides the only way to preserve contentment and prevent "as long as you are happy" from becoming a contradiction.

My mother excavates the green lives carefully. Plodding along, she ensures that their fragile stems are unbroken and fully unearthed. Whether I'll be excavating a site or digging in another, I'll search for lives which have waited thousands of years to surface. I hope to preserve another sort of life, through a tolerance for the slow deliberate motions of weeding, worthy perhaps of even more patience, because it results in a greater permanence.

Crossword Puzzles and M&Ms

Jennifer McNamee
Spring 1996 – Volume XVII

Growing up, I've always associated thoughts of my Uncle Neal with my grandmother's house. That was where he belonged, and fit in as naturally as the furniture – "This is my grandfather's chair, my grandmother's lamp, my Uncle Neal." I accepted the presence of a grown man sharing the home of my grandparents with the willingness of a young child. It was not until I had grown older and joined the dinner table for the post-meal "coffee talk," that the oddity of my Uncle Neal's presence, and the stories accompanying it, came to me in bits and pieces. The gradual relation of his bizarre history lent insight to his curious behavior, and brought me to the realization that although our relationship is shrouded in mystery, he remains a solid and gentle figure in my life. My love for him goes beyond the obligatory love that one has for a family member, and much like Uncle Neal himself, it relies on none of society's delegated norms. My friendship with him is not based on shared experience, comforting advice, or hours of pleasant conversation. It exists solely through an unstated compassion that I have held for him since I was a little girl.

A year older than my grandfather, Uncle Neal is a thin man who has to bend down slightly to receive my kiss on his cheek. His days are quiet, habitual and solitary. His plaid shirts, bought through the Sears Catalog, are faithfully ironed. When he isn't diligently nursing the tulips or tomatoes to life, he is working his way through a daily crossword. After eating, he disappears into the darkness of his room and is not seen or heard from for the remainder of the evening. Even on days when family gatherings take place, Uncle Neal confines himself to the safety of his familiar walls. Although as a child I never saw anything peculiar about his lack of participation, I often missed him. Creeping up the stairs to his room, I would push my small finger through the crack under his door in a gesture of hello. He would call back "Hello" in a low, muffled voice, but he never opened the door to let me in. I often took his decision to remain removed from the family personally, as though my inability to draw him out of his shell was some form of failure. His realm was impenetrable, and my friendly gestures did not hold the power to convince him he was welcome at our table. I didn't recognize that his unwillingness to leave the comfort of his room was not due to any form of failure on my part. Rejected, I would climb back down the stairs in my patent leather shoes to join the rest of my family.

When explaining Uncle Neal to others, my family and I always use the word "hermit" with a tone of endearment, and smile at the peculiarity that he lends to our lives. Removed from phone calls and other social gatherings, Uncle Neal's life is a quiet routine that differs from my family's bustling closeness. His lifestyle deviates from what society had taught me to accept as "normal." The reason for his isolation was explained to me by my grandmother over hot tea and cheesecake shortly before I entered high school. Uncle Neal is not my true uncle – he is not blood related. His entry into my family began with his engagement to my grandmother's sister, Mary. Young and full of life, she was supposed to have been an odd, but suitable compliment to a quiet young man who worked hard, saved well, and kept to himself a bit too much. She brought him "out into the light," – somewhere he was afraid to go on his own. Their future was bright and hopeful, and looked on favorably by all of my family. A week before the wedding, Mary was killed in a trolley accident that left her younger brother seriously injured. They buried her, and my uncle Neal's dreams on their scheduled wedding day.

The brisk, matter-of-fact nature with which my grandmother related this story left me bewildered. No matter how often I hear it, I find myself looking upon my Uncle Neal with sorrowful awe, and wanting somehow to comfort him. An imaginative child, I like to romanticize his existence, rationalizing his chosen detachment from my life by placing him in a Shakespearean tragedy where he wanders through life alone, living only for the day that he can be reunited with his love. Even though I respect my uncle's lifestyle, not knowing whether it was a matter of choice disturbs me.

His moving in with my grandparents is something I don't quite remember. It wasn't so much an event as a subtle coming-to-be. Although a perfectly healthy young man with a job at the Breyer's ice cream factory across the bridge in Philadelphia, an elder sister to turn to, and a life full of opportunities ahead, my Uncle Neal moved into an extra room in the home of my great-grandmother. He lived there until she grew so frail that she had to pack her belongings and take up residence with her elder daughter, Jane – my grandmother. Jane inherited Uncle Neal along with the rosaries, lamp shades, and perfume bottles her mother brought along.

And so the *quiet shadow* came to live under their roof, and he fills his days with four o'clock meals, seven o'clock baths, and piles of *National Geographic* – read, examined, and memorized. He has a habit of meticulously obtaining knowledge, only to store it away in his mind. He is a fountain of knowledge but shares little of it. My uncle walks through the rooms of the house with a careful, determined step, keeping his wisdom, life, and inspirations to himself. His love is gently brushed upon my brother, sister and myself, on birthdays and Christmas, not in brightly wrapped packages, cards, or even verbal explanations, but in the form of a three pound bag of M&M's and a twenty dollar bill folded and placed in a small, plain envelope. When I was younger, and still in grammar school, it was difficult for me to accept such a gift – handed over without any terms of endearment – as a gift of love. It took me a long time to recognize that the absence of fancy words, or warm hugs and wishes, was not a sign of detachment. Rather, it was a gesture so simple, and so pure that it could only mirror the warmest of intentions. In the decades that he has been a part of my family, the three of us are the only ones ever to have received a gift of any sort from him.

Uncle Neal has remained a true constant throughout my life. Even his appearance and demeanor have held their continuity. He never married, dated, or left the shelter of our small town. That is why the night we were forced to report him as a missing person was so terrifying, and so bizarre that we could not help but find it funny. At half past nine on a school night during my senior year, my grandmother – frightened – called to report that when she had come home my Uncle Neal and his once gray, and slightly battered '76 Chevy, were missing. Three hours later he still hadn't returned. He was the type of man whose schedule you could time yourself by, and had he ever been out past sunset in the fourteen years she had lived with him, there might have been no need for concern. After all, a sixty-five year old man should be able to take care of himself. There was no message left with my grandfather, and no reason for him to be gone, not even a possible destination. The food shopping had been done only two days before, and he had no friends to speak of – not that he would have visited them anyway. Uncle Neal was lost, and we were frightened.

My uncle's privacy is very important to him, and it is respected at all costs. Because of this my grandmother was afraid to enter his room. In all the years they have shared a home, she had never gone past his doorway. Despite my grandmother's hollow protests, my mother sent me up to Uncle Neal's room in order to search for clues – names, phone numbers, addresses – as to where he might have gone, while she got on the phone with the police station. Entering the forbidden room, I was tempted to snoop around. A thin quilt adorned his bed, and his shelves were piled high with neat stacks of *National Geographic* and *Reader's Digest*. His closet doors were shut, and there wasn't a single mirror. The lighting was poor. A small bedside lamp and a reading light, its arm bent over his reading chair, were barely enough to illuminate the room. It had the hushed, dusty air of an old library where the silence envelops you, and the surrounding refuses you welcome, making lingering about rather uncomfortable.

What fascinated me the most was his desk. Located in the corner of the room, the large mass was littered with piles of papers that did not fit in the drawers. Pinned above his desk was a faded construction-paper bookcover, written in my scribbled, grade school hand. It touched me to know that he had held onto something dear, something I had long forgotten. In his desk drawer, I found a card holder (containing the numbers of two dozen people that he might have found important, many of them employers that he hadn't worked for in over twenty years), snuggled between several piles of bills – fives, tens, and twenties nearly five inches tall. He had never trusted banks and his money lay in piles, like these, stashed throughout the room. Like the countless tidbits of knowledge he had gathered, the bills remained useless because he didn't have a means of sharing or applying them.

When I returned downstairs, it was awkward relating to the police officer our concern over a grown man who was out past ten o'clock. We spent forty minutes explaining, describing, and worrying in front of the policeman. And no sooner had he filled out the paper work and released a description of Uncle Neal over the radio, did the gray Chevy pull into the driveway. Uncle Neal entered the house a bit sheepishly, and was quite surprised to find a policeman waiting in his living room. He quietly explained to us that after ten years of turning down birthday invitations from a particular relative of his, he had decided to accept, and make the hour and a half drive down to see him. He also mumbled to the police officer that it was indeed out of character for him, and that we were not out of line to show concern. Then he shuffled past us towards his bedroom. Apparently, there was nothing more to be said. It was this abrupt explanation of the situation that my family found itself recounting with gentle laughter over tea later that night. No matter how long we mulled over the night's happenings, we could not understand what had motivated Uncle Neal, after a decade of isolation, to travel to Delaware.

My family had taken for granted the predictability of my uncle's lifestyle. We failed to acknowledge this separate piece of him which in fact heightened the mystery.

His disappearance exemplifies better than any of my words possibly could, the mystique surrounding my Uncle Neal. He is a man who chooses silence, a man who values privacy and solitude. There was no justification for his leaving, and no explanations. My uncle is a puzzle to me. But, the distance between us, the lack of words have never destroyed the affection that I have for him. He hides everything about himself – his money, his knowledge, and his emotions, making the smallest offering from him a gift of gold. My love for Uncle Neal – like his coming to be a part of my family – is a subtle but important part of my life. His unusual behavior makes him who he is – it lends itself to laughter and good will that I will always associate with my grandmother's home.

Nothing Gold Can Stay

Jessica Wolf
Spring 1996 – Volume XVII

> Nature's first green is gold,
> Her hardest hue to hold.
> Her early leaf's a flower;
> But only so an hour.
> Then leaf subsides to leaf.
> So Eden sank to grief.
> So dawn goes down to day,
> Nothing gold can stay.
> – *Robert Frost*

"Will you help me with this morphine patch, hon?"

Gary sits next to me on my uncle's back patio in a white wicker chair. It is late August, a surprisingly cool evening for Georgetown. I hesitate, my hand poised over a platter of chilled steamed shrimp and spicy cocktail sauce. My Uncle Chris always goes all out for our family and friend get togethers. This evening it is my father and stepmother Ellen, myself, Chris's lover, Scott, and Gary – no longer just a college friend of Chris's, but more of a family member. "I need this new patch to go on my left shoulder blade where the other one is," Gary explains quietly, careful to keep our conversation between us. "The other one has run out of medicine and I'm starting to feel not so terrific. I was hoping I'd be able to make it through this evening without having to inconvenience anyone."

Uncle Chris introduced Gary to our family on Thanksgiving five years ago. He had no family in the D.C. area, so he spent the evening with us. Although I had just met Gary, it seemed that he already knew a great deal about me.

"Chris tells me that you were just in a musical," he said.

"Yeah – I was in *Guys and Dolls* last month at school."

"Well, I was looking through my albums, and I found the original version of the soundtrack, so I taped it for you." Gary extended a tan and muscular arm. "I thought you might enjoy it." Simple gestures like that were what impressed me most about Gary – I hadn't known this man for more than a few hours and he was already doing nice things.

"Do you need another Coke Jess? Another club soda Gary?" my father asks from the bar at the other end of the patio where he, Chris, Scott, and my stepmother are making plans for a weekend getaway to New York.

"I'm doing fine, John," Gary says. "Thanks for asking." I shake my head. Gary extends the patch towards me. It is shaped like an extra-large Band-Aid, the kind that is the right size for when you scrape your knee as a child. It is clear like a jellyfish. I stare at it, then at Gary's arm. There is a lesion on the underside of his forearm, purple in color. His arm is bone-thin and pale. I take the patch of morphine and Gary unbuttons his yellow oxford shirt so that I can get to his back. My stepmother and father look over from the far side of the patio. My uncle, bringing out stuffed mushrooms from inside, stops in the doorway when he sees Gary removing his shirt. Scott looks down at the brick floor. I am afraid to make eye contact with any of them, sure that if the pain is reflected in their eyes, I will cry.

When Uncle Chris and Scott introduced us to Gary, he was HIV positive. Today, as I peel the backing off this sticky square of potent medicine, Gary is dying of AIDS.

I am conscious of my fingers on Gary's back, pressing gently on the patch. I know that morphine is used for patients in extreme pain, and I wonder how Gary is feeling. My parents and uncle have gone back to jabbering about New York, and I am stunned that they can concentrate on anything other than Gary, his patch, and the marks allover his back, chest, and stomach. "So are you getting excited about going back to school in a week?" Gary asks. He buttons his shirt up and sits back in the chair. "Thanks for helping me with that."

I feel like I'll cry if I try to speak. This man is dying, but is capable of small talking about college. "Yeah, it will be nice to get back down to Washington and Lee."

"You'll really enjoy your sophomore year Jess. That was my favorite year," he says. He grimaces with the pain. "The patch hasn't kicked in yet. Anyway, I hope I get the opportunity to come visit you at school again this year."

"I hope so too."

The previous year, my nineteenth birthday fell during the first semester of my freshman year. My stepmother and father had come down to school to surprise me, bringing Gary and my uncle with them. I spent the weekend showing them around campus and introducing them to my friends. I was able to find a few minutes alone with Gary to thank him for coming to celebrate my birthday.

"It means a lot that you would drive all the way down here just to celebrate my birthday," I said. We were walking down one of the side streets in Lexington. It was uncharacteristically warm for early November, and Gary had his sleeves rolled up. I did not notice any lesions that day. "It makes me feel good to know that you'd drive four hours to see me when I'm just your friend's niece."

"Jessica, let me tell you something," he said, looking directly into my eyes. "Eighteen years ago, I moved out here from Minnesota, leaving behind a twin brother and his baby girl Cary, my niece. I was fortunate enough to meet Chris, who I love like a brother. And in knowing Chris, I have acquired a whole new family – your dad, Ellen, Scott, and you, another niece. I would drive across the country for your birthday."

"I'm glad that you're here this weekend for my birthday, and that you're a part of my life and my family Gary."

"Me too hon. I just wish we could have met sooner."

Sophomore year, two months after seeing Gary at Uncle Chris's, I receive a postcard. On the front are hydrangeas, and Gary has written: "Be nice to flowers." Flowers and plants are Gary's assurance that there is a God. I learned this when I went to visit him at his house in Georgetown during the spring of my freshman year, shortly after my grandfather had died. His small backyard was completely packed with sunflowers, tulips, zinnias, hibiscus, and about a million other plants that I didn't know the names of. "These remind me that life continues on and that God is watching," he said pointing to the vibrant splashes of color in front of us. "Your grandfather is in good hands hon. I promise." That was how Gary was, finding beauty and comfort in the face of death.

My eyes linger on the front of the postcard and I am afraid to turn it over, afraid of what I might find. I am hoping that on the back of the postcard I will find the words: "I'M CURED!" Instead I find: "Sorry I will not make it for your birthday. I am in Miami for some rest and relaxation. I think of you often. Love, Gary." The handwriting is shaky. I have a terrible feeling in the pit of my stomach that Gary won't ever make it home. I call my father in Baltimore. "When did Gary go to Florida?" I ask.

My father sighs on the other end of the telephone. "Gary's not feeling so hot, Jess. He left about a week ago and is going to stay down there with some friends as long as he can."

"So he's staying there until he starts to die?" Tears stream down my face and I choke on my sobs. "I want to see him. I want to see him again."

This was not supposed to happen to Gary. Gary was the one who brought flowers to my stepmother and me whenever we got together for brunch or a dinner; the one who kicked me under the table to let me know that he was as bored as I was when Chris and my father would discuss their cases; the one who watched football with me on New Year's Day while the rest of the family was in the living room, wishing they were the ones in the den watching TV.

I am able to see him again. Gary comes home from Miami for Christmas. He comes with Chris and Scott to our house Christmas morning. His face looks sunken and his eyes far away. I feel like I am looking at a skeleton with just the thinnest layer of skin stretched miserably over it.

"My firm didn't invite me to their Christmas party," he tells my family. He has already talked this over with Chris and Scott numerous times. "They didn't invite me because I have AIDS." The five of us, his family, have no words to make things right.

I am sitting next to Gary on the loveseat as he tells us this, playing with the soft material of my skirt. My eyes fill with tears so that everything is blurred like opening them underwater at the ocean. Uncle Chris suggests that we exchange presents, uncomfortable with the silence. Gary gives me a red ribbon pin. I give Gary a coffee table book about gardening. He slowly flips through the book and says, "Life is truly breathtaking. What's in this book makes me believe that God is up there watching out for us."

I often think back to that night in August on my uncle's patio. Before that night, AIDS was just an acronym for a new disease, an issue, something that I read about in *Newsweek* or heard about on television. Although Gary had been infected with the HIV virus the entire five years that I had known him, that night in August was my first exposure to anyone who had contracted the virus, someone with full-blown AIDS – this was somebody I loved.

I knew about the horror of dying with AIDS. That same summer I watched a public television program on the disease. It was a documentary about two men who were both diagnosed with the virus. The movie charted the course of their relationship and the progression of their disease. I watched the two men lose weight, lose their hair; next came the development of lesions. As a couple they grew weak, then died. Seeing Gary on the patio that night I knew that he would die the same way.

It amazed me that Gary could wake up each morning knowing that he had a disease that was destroying him. I found it difficult to get out of bed in the morning simply to turn a paper in for class, or because I was fighting with my boyfriend the night before. I could not comprehend what someone would have to possess in order to continue fighting, knowing the end is a losing battle.

Gary had already lost his lover to AIDS a year prior to my meeting him. The question of how Gary caught the HIV virus was never asked. I always assumed that he had caught it through homosexual sex because his lover died of the disease. The likelihood of this being true never affected me – I wasn't homophobic. My uncle was gay, and this never disturbed me. My father and stepmother were also very supportive of Chris's sexuality. They acknowledged Scott as Chris's partner and treated them as a couple. Despite all of this, I grew up fairly tolerant of homosexual humor. Behind their backs, Chris and Scott became "Uncle Chris and Aunt Scott" to my father, stepmother, and I. I guess that is the way my family dealt with the situation. If you had asked me at the time, I would have sworn to you that I was one-hundred percent sympathetic about homosexuality.

Then I put a morphine patch on my dying friend's back.

A couple of nights after I received Gary's postcard, I was at school watching MTV with some of my friends at a fraternity house. They showed a clip of Axl Rose wearing a T-shirt that mimicked the Raid commercial (Raid: Kills Bugs Dead). His shirt said "AIDS: Kills Fags Dead." Most of the people in the room started laughing. One of my friends yelled out: "Those fucking faggots deserve it!"

Back in July of that summer, before I put a morphine patch on my friend's lesion-covered back, I probably would have laughed at the joke on the T-shirt. I also would have let the comment go. I no longer found it funny. "You're a bunch of ignorant fucks!" I shouted. I stormed out of the room to the question: "What are you, some kind of fucking dyke?"

I was not on a mission to change people's minds about homosexuality. I didn't expect my friends or my conservative school community to have an epiphany and embrace homosexuality. I just wanted someone to make the pain go away. I wanted AIDS to disappear. I wanted Gary to live. Deep down I knew that this wasn't going to happen. Those horrible words, "Those fucking faggots deserve it!" rang in my ears. When I heard the word AIDS, I thought of Gary. When homophobic individuals heard the word AIDS, it seemed they believed the disease was punishment, retribution. It made me sick to think that to some people, Gary deserved to have AIDS. To me Gary was simply a dear friend with a terminal disease, whose position in society was complicated by the prejudice against him.

This past August, almost exactly a year from my last visit with Gary, I was able to be with him during the final weeks of his life. He was in a hospice in Maryland. Most of his hair was gone and he couldn't have weighed more than ninety pounds. The only forms of nourishment he could take in were sherbet and ginger ale – otherwise, he was fed from an IV.

He could barely focus his eyes due to the morphine and opium the doctors were giving him. He drooled. In his worst moments he would hallucinate, crying out that snakes were falling from the ceiling. He was afraid of pain. He looked just like the two men from the AIDS documentary, except that Gary was a part of my life – not a television personality. He was still Gary somewhere inside his deteriorating body. I sat often by his bed before he died. I held his hand and told him that I loved him. He told me that he loved me too, and loved being a part of my family. I told him that I had learned a lot about courage from him. He told me that it had nothing to do with courage, that he was living the life that was chosen for him. There came a point when he couldn't speak, and his eyes remained shut for hours. As I watched him approach the end of his struggling, I told him that I would always associate him with gardens – beautiful, rich colored flowers and greenery, pushing and straining upward from the stubborn soil.

Waking Up to the Bomb

Rana Malek

Spring 1997 – Volume XVIII

"Oh shit, please don't let it be the Arabs." My prayer to any existing deity escaped my lips as I heard on the radio that a federal building in Oklahoma City had been destroyed by a car bomb. As soon as the nineteen casualties were mentioned, the NPR report moved on to say that "three Middle Eastern-looking men were seen driving away from the scene."

The rest of my day became dedicated to the bombing. On the news, pictures of dead children were being flashed, horrifying those who saw them. Reports of a Jordanian-American being detained in London's airport were mentioned almost simultaneously with the death count.

The atmosphere in my house was somber that evening, more so than in a lot of other homes. When my dad came home, we were told that if we went to school the next day, we shouldn't take part in the discussion of the bombing, shouldn't attract any more attention to ourselves than needed. It was temping not to go to school, and I wouldn't have been alone if I hadn't, because many other Arab-American parents kept their kids home from school the day after the bombing.

I went to school though, because I was naïve. My school was quite multiracial and we never had skinheads marching in the hallways. I never really felt at odds because of my heritage. Sure there was the awkward period during Desert Storm, when anti-Arab hate crimes increased by 300% in a year, but I never confronted the attitude I was forced to face in the wake of the Oklahoma City bombing.

That day in school was unbelievable. I had never hid my heritage from anyone, because I had never felt the need. After four years, my classmates knew a lot about me and I knew a lot about them. That was the one day in my life that I wanted to make my heritage go away. In my AP classes, Oklahoma City was brought up, and as people shared their hurt and outrage, many cautious glances were thrown in my direction. The discussion focused more around the perpetrators than on the deed. What kind of monsters could kill children, what religious cause could warrant such violence? Of course they were talking about Islam, and the monsters were Arabs. The words were carefully chosen on my behalf.

The racism didn't become truly clear until I went to International Business. It was a class I had to take for a graduation requirement, and it was a far cry from the atmosphere of my AP classes. As my teacher clicked and clacked her way into the classroom, she tossed her hair and asked, "People, is there any international news we should discuss?" Immediately the class erupted into cries of Oklahoma City. The loudest voice dominated, and we all listened as Christian shared her vast and impressive knowledge on the subject: "A bunch of Arabs blew up the building because they knew children were in there. In fact, they arrested the three Arab men who were driving away from the building this morning." Her words set off a vast array of the many Middle Eastern scholars in the room who explained how killing children was typical of Arabs, how mad they were at the government for letting "them" in the country, how they better catch those s.o.b.'s and make them pay. I watched in horror as each statement became more unveiled and more violent. I watched in horror as the teacher made no attempt to explain that no suspects existed, and I watched in horror as she nodded her head in agreement at times. She knew I was Arabic, and the rest of the class knew it too.

Somehow the day ended, and I came home to the nervousness of Janet Reno's press conference. I actually heard the first part on NPR on my way home. I had no way of seeing the sketches of the two suspects, of knowing what they looked like. As the car pulled into the garage, I ran into the house, up the stairs to the TV where my mom was watching. As the camera moved to the sketches, I grabbed my mom's knee. "Mom, they can't be Arabs, they're white!" John Doe #1 was as un-Arab as possible with his fair hair and eyes. It was such an incredibly emotional moment, my joy at the feeling of being vindicated of a crime I didn't commit, and the horror that the nation's hysteria made me experience racism up close.

I do admit that my first inclination was that the bombers were Arabs. After all, we had the World Trade Center bombing and the conspiracy by the fundamentalists led by Sheik Rahman. In addition, the Islamic world has remained somewhat of a mystery to most Americans. The press has chosen to constantly focus on the anti-American rallies and the fundamentalism. Stereotypical movies such as *True Lies* further implant the notion of missile-toting, American-hating, swarthy Muslim men, crusading for radical religion. In other words, the press finds the minority of the fastest growing religion far more interesting that the actual, scholarly, meditative religion that it is. I didn't expect America, with all these hateful images, not to have the same suspicions that I as an Arab-American had. But what scared me at first, and then infuriated me later, was what Richard Lacayo, in a Time editorial, summarized as: "For a while last week, something in the national mood appeared to be turning darkly against Arab-Americans." Damn right it was. In the time between the bombing and the flashes of Timothy McVeigh's WASP face, an Arab-American woman living in Oklahoma City suffered a miscarriage in her seventh month of pregnancy after a mob surrounded her home and threw rocks through her windows and shouted racial threats. Thousand of Arab parents kept their children at home after hysteria was instilled by people like former Congressman Dave McCurdy. On the Larry King Live show, the ex- Congressman explained that he knew Arab terrorism "could happen here." An American-Islamic convention had been held in Oklahoma City and the presence of Muslims, according to McCurdy, was proof enough that Arab terrorism could happen in Oklahoma City. In a Newsweek editorial, Jonathan Alter sums up McCurdy's influence: "McCurdy...Got the anti-Arab finger-pointing going early by sounding on TV as if he knew what he was talking about; he didn't." So many "Middle Eastern experts" fed growing assumptions by saying that the bombing was typical of Arab terrorists, implying that killing children was typical of Arabs.

While I would accept suspicion at an initial level, I cold not accept how, overnight, I became one of "them" and now it was the USA versus "them." My belief that a group is not judged by the actions of a few of its members came up against harsh reality in my America of those few days.

And even after Timothy McVeigh was arrested, it didn't end. Because now the line was "how can it be one of us?" It fed the notion that terrorism and crime are a foreign import, when in reality America is crime's capital. Alter, in the editorial, defined the emotions of the country best when he writes, "Who can deny that it would have been emotionally easier if foreigners had done it? Had 'they' been responsible, as so many suspected, the grief and anger could have been channeled against a fixed enemy, uniting the country as only an external threat can do…And if we couldn't identify a country to bomb, at least we could have the comfort of knowing that the depravity of the crime – its subhuman quality – was the product of another culture unfathomably different from our own." In other words, my culture would be so much easier to associate with depravity. How am I supposed to swallow that? A culture that I associate with warmth and family and history becomes a culture of terrorists instead. We choose to accept this stereotype because it is so much easier, because to actually learn the culture would be far more difficult. It also would be so much more difficult to learn that Arab doesn't equal evil and terrorism. It is a choice of ignorance that many make, many educated and liberal minds included.

A few hours after Reno's conference, my sister called from Italy, where she was finishing her junior year of college. It was amazing that even though she was in Italy and wasn't facing what my brother, sister and I were facing here, she knew instinctively what would be going on. And that bothers me. At times I feel as though the four of us have this weird sixth sense that comes with our dark hair and dark eyes. Alia's call came with the blessing of her sarcastic humor and we joked about how the next day in school we Arab-Americans could be self-righteous for a change. And as she ended our expensive phone call, she reiterated a sentiment my parents had been constantly saying: "I am sorry you have to go through this."

What infuriates me is that they are sorry. No one else is. Why should my parents and older sister be sorry because of a heritage that I was fortunate enough to receive? I wondered why NPR wasn't sorry for their claim that Middle Eastern men drove away from the building when it turned out there was no source to back up the claim, and in fact, it was nothing but a rumor. I think my friend, Dan, who spoke in my place during that awful International Business class, summed it up when he asked: "What does it mean to look Middle Eastern? Because if it is dark hair and dark eyes, I have both and I'm not Arabic; and what about Greeks, and Italians, and Spaniards? They're all dark." And he was really right. How in the world do we pass judgment on people's ethnicities, as NPR did, on no definite source and a glance from a passing vehicle? There is a great deal of danger in identifying race by face. After all, it was the slanted eyes of the Japanese that forced them into placement camps during World War Two.

I had assumed the vindication of the Arab race would put an end to the problem. I could go to school, make a couple of remarks about how quick everyone was to judge and the whole situation would be over. In reality, it wasn't.

The bombing brought to light a decision I had to make, as to whether I would accept my heritage as an Arab-American, or to take the stance my brother had. He decided that even though my parents were Syrian, we, the kids, had no association with their heritage. We, his sisters, call him the same name he goes by in school, Sam, while my parents call him by his birth name, Hussam. He never discusses or publicizes his heritage the way my sister and I do. But I have come to realize that Sam's position has been built up as a protection of sorts. He doesn't want to be forced into a group, a stereotype based on his birthright. And it's a path that many kids of ethnic backgrounds choose. And I do think that my brother didn't feel the effects of the bombing as much as I did, because his classmates had no real insight into his heritage.

But I came to find a flaw in his stance as well. No

matter how much we choose to deny our past, it really does catch up with us. Because whenever I, or my brother, meet someone, our names automatically kick in that something is different. Eventually people wind up asking about your heritage, and no matter how born, bred, and true to the USA you are, that heritage becomes quite visible. So I have come to realize that I have this choice, to simply deal with the situation whenever it arises and pray to God that it never does, or that I can find something that makes me proud enough that I can fight the stereotypes that are going to be thrown at me.

The Oklahoma Bombing has forced me to reevaluate many of my assumptions. I have the complex dilemma of trying to balance the fact that I hate some of the beliefs of my culture and the fact that I am still bonded and respect that culture in a thousand and one ways. I used to differentiate myself by my religion: I was Christian, while most Arabs were Muslim. But that really means nothing especially since Arab equals Muslim in this society. I found myself needing to understand a religion that I had brushed aside as not being important. I found myself dedicating so much time to reading anything I could on Islam. After all, how can we defend or insult something of which we know so little? Interestingly enough, my older sister decided to write her junior thesis on women and Islam. Even though we were separated by ocean and country, each one of us was triggered into understanding something of which we had only surface knowledge. For me, it was the fact that Oklahoma City proved that in some way, I would always be tied to my heritage. After all, chances are if something gets blown up, we will again assume it is Arabs, and I need to be prepared to face that. As for my sister, she found herself in a country that lived completely differently from the lifestyle of the Middle East, yet at the same time the sense of judgment did not exist in comparison to the USA.

Even after this searching, we both reached the same conclusions. Our relationship with this religion that so drastically affects our culture is complex. As two feminist women, we find that we are one of the first to defend Islam when it is insulted, and one of the first to critique the religion when it is evaluated by our Muslim friends. One could argue that there is no real sense to our thoughts, that we haven't reached a conclusion at all. However, after our probing and research, I think we both can defend and critique the religion far better than before Oklahoma City and her year in Italy. Truly there is some comfort in being knowledgeable about this religion. When the religion and its followers are attacked, I can tell when it is justifiable or not. I know when the truth is used for the attack, or when the truth is altered to fit devious minds. In all honestly, I don't really want to champion this cause, but I do not want to deal with the stereotypes resulting from ignorance. It is not possible to reap the benefits without being a part of the fight. I never want to go through the Oklahoma City experience again. I don't want my sisters and brother to ever have to suffer a minute of racism if I can help it. This is the only way.

The past is the past, and I can't change it or its aftermath on my heritage, but I will not allow the actions of a few to be the only representation of my culture to America. That is cheap and dangerous. America didn't deserve the hysteria that malicious minds created in the wake of the Oklahoma City bombing. The anger and hatred directed against Arab-Americans faded too rapidly after the identification of the actual perpetrator. The wrath that could have bombed any Middle Eastern country was silent against the blond hair and blue eyes of Timothy McVeigh. It is frightening to contemplate where it went. Is it that we can't hate our own as much as we can others? Or is the anger waiting for the next opportunity to rear its ugly head? I don't know, and I am afraid to wonder. But from now and until that time, if it ever comes, I just might be able to do something. It just took a car bomb and racism to get me to see that.

It's a Small World After All...

Joseph Truong
Spring 1997 – Volume XVIII

A few years back, I was at Keleti railway station in Budapest, chatting with a young Belgian girl and her Swedish friend while we were waiting for a train to whisk us off to Bulgaria for a week. Budapest was one of the last stops we'd make before arriving in Bulgaria, where a world youth conference was being held. My two friends had just finished attending another congress which ended a few days earlier in Zalaegerszeg, a city to the west of Budapest. We were having a great time comparing our observations and adventures up to that point. Of course, we did this all in Esperanto...

Many Americans have never heard of Esperanto. Esperanto is that "joke" language of the media, mentioned when a comedian needs new material, or when Murphy Brown wants to be truly sarcastic. For others, it was a novelty from the 1920s, after World War I when everyone was so eager to promote world peace and understanding, long before the rise of the United States and, thus, of English. Some applaud the basic idea, but think it is too obscure to ever receive recognition (thus the plethora of songs referring to Esperanto, by alternative bands such as They Might Be Giants, Shadowfax and Prefab Sprout). Yet Esperanto is neither a joke nor a thing of the past. Despite what everyone may believe (or may want to believe), it is still being used and is in fact thriving across the globe.

The word "Esperanto" literally means "one who

hopes" in the language itself. It was taken from a modest book published in 1887 in Warsaw, Poland, the work of one man, Dr. Ludovic Zamenhof. Having grown up in Bialystok (in present-day Poland) which was the home of Russians, Germans, Jews and Poles, he recognized how ethnic tensions among the four groups were only made more salient by their differences in language. This small city in Eastern Europe mirrored the world, one fractured by a multitude of languages just as the Tower of Babel documented.

Although sharing a neutral language would not in itself automatically bring world peace, it would, Zamenhof thought, at least reduce the tensions that existed by facilitating communication, something which the world has always needed. But what was meant by "neutral"? Few, especially Americans, ever realize the politics of language. While I was attending a youth conference at the United Nations this past summer, this became cruelly clear.

According to the United Nations, nearly 80% of the world's youth live in the lesser – and least developed – countries (which before were known as the "Third World" nations), but practically none of the delegates of these nations ever contributed to the dealings at the conference; the majority of the views presented came from European or North American voices.

The entire conference was held in English alone, because the United Nations lacked money to interpret into other languages. Unfortunately, many of the participants could not speak English adequately enough to keep up with the rapid-fire happenings of the conference. Some did speak Spanish or Portuguese, yet even they were excluded in the conversations by the English-only chats.

Here we were, trying to deal with the problems of the world's youth, and the representatives of the majority of the global youth community could not even understand what we were doing to help them. If the United Nations could not afford interpretation for the event into Spanish or Portuguese (languages which are widely known and spoken), what were we to do with those persons who spoke lesser-known languages?

Basically, if you didn't speak English, you weren't included at the United Nations. It was that simple. Should those in economic power force everyone else in the world to speak their language simply because it serves their needs? How is it that the few with economic power can dictate the wills of the many? Why shouldn't everyone speak Chinese, the world's most spoken language in terms of population, or Hindi, the first runner-up for this title?

Esperanto was created exactly to surpass that. While it may look and sound like other languages, it is not linked with any language or with any specific country; an "Esperantoland" does not exist. Esperanto can be heard and spoken as much in Washington as in Moscow, Dar-es Salaam as in Copenhagen. No country can lay claim to Esperanto as being "its" language, and thus using it helps speakers take off their political jackets and simply communicate with each other. People learn it without feeling that they are somehow giving up their own native tongues, or unconsciously showing the importance of another. Politically, Esperanto has no strings attached.

Esperanto must be considered a success after its more than 100 years of existence. A respectable number of people (estimates run the gamut from two to six million) still speak it, without any institution or army to enforce its use, nor any economic powerhouse to support it. Esperantists can be found in 110 nations, with national organizations in 80 of them. There exist Esperantist literature (original and translated), periodicals, music, clubs (with subjects from agriculture to Quakerism to yoga), radio stations (which included, for a short period of time in the '60s, the

United States' own foreign broadcast system, the Voice of America)…it is used just as any other language would be used.

While a variety of renowned personalities either spoke or supported Esperanto, from Leo Tolstoi (who wrote the first play in Esperanto, in 1896) and Mark Twain, to Alfred Fried (winner of the Nobel peace Prize) and Pope John Paul II, the reason that the language has survived is that it is accessible to the common person. For each famous person who speaks or supports the language, there are probably hundreds of "normal" people using it in their lives.

Zamenhof, in having the ability to "construct" a more ideal language, had a few goals in mind, all to help make the language simple and uncomplicated.

A primary concern was making it consistent throughout – any grammatical rule once made would be applied everywhere in Esperanto. No exceptions. Anyone who has tortured themselves with irregular verbs, tables of adjective endings and such will immediately see the results of such an improvement.

Nouns end in –*o*, adjectives in –*a*, and adverbs in –*e*. Plurals are formed by adding a –*j* to the end of the word. Infinitives end in –*i*, while simple tense endings are -*as* (present), -*is* (past) and –*os* (future). The same grammatical points which take students years to understand in other languages have just been summarized into four lines in Esperanto. Another two or three years of study could be eliminated by the following reminder: there are no exceptions to the rule. All nouns end in –*o*, all verbs are conjugated alike…few other languages can say that.

Since it was intended for a global audience, Zamenhof likewise had to be considerate of not only other Europeans, but also of those on other continents and other linguistic families. The finished language, according to Pierre Janton in his book *Esperanto: Language, Literature and Community*, has a vocabulary in which 75% of the "root" words come from Romance languages (primarily Latin and French), 20% from Germanic languages (which includes English), and the remaining from Greek, Slavic languages, and a variety of other languages.

Anyone flipping through an Esperanto dictionary would be able to notice this unique festival of words from different languages. Even without the translations, English-speakers would be able to guess a large amount of the words: *letero, familio, somero, birdo* (plurals would, of course, be *leteroj, familioj, someroj, birdoj*). Fortunately for us English-speakers, some other important words are based on English: for example, the word for "yes" is *jes*, but pronounced exactly the same. The pronoun "I" is *mi* (pronounced as "me"), and "she" is *si* (pronounced like "she" itself).

A final consideration was that the language's grammar be functional for everybody. One example is word order. In English, we've been drilled with the "subject-verb-object" structure of sentences; however, not every language has that basic order. To accommodate this problem, nouns used in the object function end in *-n*. This allows the speaker to switch the position of the words to one with which he or she is comfortable. For example, making a sentence around the verb *skribi* (to write):

Mi skribas la leteron.
I write the letter.
means the same as
Skribas mi la leteron, or *La leteron mi skribas.*

To someone who just learned a little about the language within the past few minutes, the last two sentences may appear to be totally different from the first. Yet, because the object ending (*-n*) affects only the word *letter*, a speaker of

Esperanto would immediately recognize that *I* am doing the writing, regardless of wherever the word may actually appear in the sentence.

While there is no one "perfect" sounding example of Esperanto, according to Zamenhof, it should sound roughly like Italian or Spanish. All the consonants are generally pronounced as in English, while the vowels should sound like what we'd call "short" vowels (ah-eh-ee-oh-oo, if you couldn't remember). So, the first sentence would sound like (mee skree-bahs lah leh-teh-rohn). Of course, it's terribly difficult to put sounds onto paper, but it nevertheless gives an approximate feel to the language.

This rough introduction to Esperanto grammar is obviously meant to give only the bare essentials of the language, but it should be enough to allow comparisons to be made with other languages. There are other more technical bits and pieces which must be studied as well, but some of the more characteristic grammatical points do show the differences between it and other languages.

Because it has a simple, "no-exceptions-to-the-rule" grammar, a vocabulary which is created and structured logically, and a pronunciation which is always consistent, many have managed to learn the language well not only through classes and course study, but also through books and correspondence courses.

This free and open access to the language via sources outside formal institutions has made the biggest difference in the world in spreading Esperanto to all classes of people, particularly those in lesser-developed countries. English in these countries is highly-prized not only because English-speaking inhabitants can gain access to the more-developed countries such as the United States and Canada through it, but also because it is a language which is generally restricted to those with the power and money, who can afford to learn it through expensive classes.

Being able to learn Esperanto through books and correspondence courses enables those who normally would not have an opportunity to learn any other language know one which will also help them access the world. The recent increase of Esperanto-speakers in Africa has supported this idea, since young people there, who would not be able to afford a course at a university or high school, can still learn the language though books sent as donations from European or North American clubs, or through correspondence courses.

I'm no exception to teaching myself the language. I learned the language through a book which I borrowed from the local public library when I was twelve. I continued borrowing it over the course of the next six months, and within that time I had taught myself a rudimentary knowledge of the language. Of course, as with any language, it takes quite a few years of experience and use to reach a stylistic flair which is a sign of a respectable speaker of a language.

At first, I didn't really know what I was getting into: I was always interested in languages, so casually reading here and there about the language kept my interest alive. But what exactly would make people want to learn Esperanto? According to Sybil Harlow, who is the current secretary of the United States Young Esperantist Organization, the reason comes from the attitude that some people have. "I think that most people who learn Esperanto are very interested in what is going on around the world (very anti-isolationist)," she said.

Sooner or later, that was the same conclusion to which I came. Because of the immense global opportunities which Esperanto offered (particularly to someone who lived in ho-hum Lancaster, Pennsylvania), it would be impossible for someone not to gain an understanding and acceptance of the cultures and peoples of the world.

I also discovered that those who speak Esperanto share a special connection and attitude, one which transcends the superficial boundaries which may tangle others, such as nationality and ethnic background. Considering the reason behind the creation of the language and in light of everything Zamenhof did to accomplish that, Esperantists try to maintain a sense of respect and tolerance for others, and treat each other as equals.

For example, the internationality of the language helps Esperantists learn to accept that there is no Esperanto accent. Yugoslavs are said to speak the "clearest" Esperanto, but no one really has a perfect Esperanto accent. Although one's grammar and pronunciation may be better than another's, his or her native accent is not considered a help or a hindrance.

This comes in contrast to what we, as native English-speakers, have accustomed ourselves. Simple accents do a great deal to separate even those with a common tongue. As native English-speakers from the United States, we are sometimes considered among the "models" of what English should sound like; English speakers in the world are rated relative to us.

We look with favor on the British when they speak because their accent is so charming and "quaint." Speaking with a British accent is even considered a sign of education, high culture and civility.

A person just as educated and high cultured who happens to speak in a Spanish accent is not as easily accepted. Hearing an accent which doesn't compare with ours (especially one which denotes a culture unfortunately looked down upon), Americans will be quick to distinguish him from the Brit as not being quite as educated, or as coming from a background of lesser status and numerous other pre-judgments, regardless of whether they are correct or not.

An example of this surfaced in the press a few months back, when an applicant of Indian background was denied a job. The prospective employer claimed it was based solely on his lack of proper qualifications, but it became evident later that this was not his only reason. The job required quite a lot of talking to clients by phone; having someone speaking with such a noticeable Indian accent would give the company a poor image. Regardless of how qualified he was, the applicant would have his accent to hold him back from certain occupations.

Yet, an even more striking example of this separation comes from my father's experiences. Maybe I'm biased because I'm his son, but I don't think my father speaks English with an accent at all. However, sometimes I've heard inconsiderate, passing comments from others about how he doesn't speak English like an American, although he has been speaking English for merely 40 years, was documented as a superior English speaker by the University of Michigan (Ann Arbor), and has been living in the United States for 20 years. It hurts to think that, despite all of these credits to his name and everything else he has done in the United States already, he could still be considered a foreigner only because he "sounds" like one.

These experiences Esperanto speakers do not have among one another, because they realize that no one in the group can claim to be a native speaker and thus naturally be superior to another. This serves to make learners of the language more confident because they can feel that they will be able to use Esperanto without being looked down upon because of something as trivial as their accent.

Yet the true reason why Esperanto has attracted and worked with even the most common people is because it enables them to reach and affect the world outside of their boundaries. Esperanto has a worldwide use which may not be as large as that of English or French, yet it reaches as many countries, if not more. The majority of these contacts happen through pen pals, periodicals, clubs, and radio broadcasts. Through each channel, anybody, regardless of background, can learn more about other cultures.

One of the best ways I've been able to truly enjoy the language has been through traveling. The Society for International Business is one of the only other campus groups which shares this wanderlust. It, too, realizes what Saint Augustine said: "The world is a book, and those who do not travel read only one page."

Esperantists tend to be very hospitable to other Esperantists, considering how relatively few there are in the world and how widely scattered they are. So, they will often offer traveling Esperantists food, a place to eat, information on the local area…in other words, host them as friends. Although this is most often done informally, there does exist an actual network, known as the *Pasporta Servo* (Passport Service), which offers a printed booklet of names and addresses of those who offer free lodging to other Esperantists.

Yet, more importantly, Esperanto gives the bewildered traveler a local contact to help make the experience a little more personal and memorable. Some people simply zip in and out of cities, with nothing more to show than photographs and tacky key rings. Esperantists pride themselves on helping others put "faces" on these cities, and letting fellow speakers leave with friendships and special memories.

While all of these trips and exchange letters and radio broadcasts may not seem to do much for world peace, they are essentially doing what Zamenhof hoped the language would accomplish – they are helping to promote world understanding. And, of course, the more we communicate and understand each other, the closer we can get to world peace. Realistically, we may never reach it, but there is no harm simply in trying.

World peace is not accomplished when countries stop fighting, or when wars end. It is very much a piecemeal miracle, one which takes place one step at a time. World peace is my experience at the National Congress of Esperanto in Hartford two years ago. I just met a young Esperantist from Uzbekistan there whose tape recorder snagged his tape. Another young person, from Cameroon, happened to walk in while I was fiddling around with it. There we were, three young people from Uzbekistan, Cameroon and the United States, trying to solve an international dilemma in Esperanto. We all understood each other and came together to find a solution. (By the way, a pair of scissors and Scotch tape eventually came to the rescue.)

When one person can understand another from a foreign culture, numerous walls come down. They come to a realization that simply being of another nationality or peoples is not enough to wage war, to murder each other, or to have resentments.

Through means such as Esperanto, peace is something which anyone can help attain. You don't have to be a world diplomat or a politician to make constructive change towards world peace. Often it is the "little persons" who can rally together to help the world.

During World War I, when communication was nearly stopped between the eastern and western fronts of Europe, the Esperantists on both sides of the war volunteered to become mail-drops for their respective cities. Anyone, regardless of whether he or she were an Esperantist or not, could give letters to the city's Esperantist delegate who would then forward it to the offices of the Universal Esperanto Association (the international coordinating body of the Esperanto movement, which was then located in Geneva, Switzerland – neutral territory). The UEA would sort the mail, then hand it off again to delegates in cities on the other side of Europe to re-deliver. This action, free out of the goodwill of the Esperantists stranded on both sides of the war, kept families and friends in contact with each other throughout the war years.

This example not only shows that anyone can aid in the peace process. It also points out that everyone is needed to help, if world peace is truly desired. It was quite important that as many Esperantists as possible helped with this project, to cover as much of the European continent as possible. Missing only one person in a certain area would mean that the system wouldn't be able to function there, causing concern to anyone with loved ones in that area.

Even a naïve young writer from Pennsylvania can help bring world peace. I was fortunate enough to experience world peace once again in Bulgaria later that summer. By some strange coincidence, some of the participants (luckily, I was one of them) bumped into each other on the streets of Sofia while waiting for our trains home. We all decided to have one last dinner together before heading back.

It was undoubtedly a magical evening. It may have been the ambiance, a lovely and elegant restaurant located in a well-preserved garden, where cats would bravely climb up the ivy-lined gates only to fall back to the ground. Maybe it was the food, the first time I had eaten something other than yogurt in nearly two weeks.

But, more than likely, it was the people who made the experience so memorable. At the last-minute banquet table which the waiters happily set up for us were seated Belgians, Germans, Dutch, Yugoslavs, French...and Americans, of course. We were all enjoying the grilled beef patties, shop-ska salad, and hearty bread while reminiscing in Esperanto about our recent experiences, joking about the "food" at the Congress, and swapping addresses. This, for me, is world peace.

I Am Only a Part

Vanessa Cisz
Spring 1997 – Volume XVIII

> "Now I fall, from dizzy heights and
> expectations, why do I hit the ground so
> hard?"
> – *The Innocence Mission*

For the first twelve years of my life, I thought that all my mother concerned herself with was baking fresh cookies, cleaning my room, and making sure that I had plenty of clean underwear. In my eyes, my mother had no brothers, no sisters; I never really understood the idea that my grandmother experienced with her daughter all of the trials and tribulations that my mother went through with me. When my mother, father, and I went back to Germany to visit family in 1990, my eyes were opened by what I saw and heard.

I missed the indications – certain things slipped out of my mother that showed she was miserable here in America (she was born, raised, and later married in Germany). We moved to America in 1987, when the Army re-stationed my father to what my mother called "the lovely little backwater state of Pennsylvania." On our first night in our new American home, she sobbed uncontrollably. I attributed this to "post-move" nerves; I did not even stop to think that she missed her real home – a small town named Klanxbull, ten minutes south of the Danish border. Never had I realized how closely she connected herself to the flat, green land that used to belong to the wild, harsh North Sea, the sheep that dotted the fresh countryside like white crests on a flat lake, or the grass covered dikes designed to prevent last century's floods. It was a part of her, a part of her that filled her with quiet comfort.

When my mother called home to Germany, it seemed to me that she always spoke to my grandmother, my Uncle Bernhard, or my Aunt Friede. She never spoke to her mother, her brother, or her sister. It never occurred to me that she had siblings upon whom she played tricks and with whom she became angry, as I did with my older brother. As soon as she spoke to her family on the phone, I left the room, for I did not understand a word of "that awful German language," as Mark Twain once described it. During my stay in Germany, my family had lived on an Army base and I attended an American school for Army children. The German instruction there was not as intense as the instruction in a regular German school, and I never really picked up the language from my German family. I suppose in leaving the room while my mother rambled on in German, I shut myself off from a side of my mother about which I did not wish to learn – that she had interests and memories to share, not all of them necessarily with me. Learning German, I felt, would have forced me to enter that world. I would then have to listen and understand the discussions that crossed the dinner table. Knowing my mother's language would bring me closer to her past life, of which I was not a part. Perhaps I was afraid of seeing and learning all of the deeper connections she had to this place. It would have hurt me to know that "I was not her whole life," and I did not want to be hurt (Friday 2).

Usually my mother and I agree on any given subject,

but about the trip in 1990, we did not. My mother was obviously excited to be going "home" for three weeks, but I remained neutral. My father was traveling with us as well; he too was excited about revisiting the place where he met and fell in love with my mother. He had not even parked the rental car in the gravel driveway when my grandmother came running out of her house, babbling in a German dialect that flowed over me and around me until it reached ears that could understand it. My mother stood up, visibly inhaled, and let a few choked cries escape. "She is glad to see her mother," I realized. "I guess I would be, too," I thought. How shallow I was, it occurs to me now; why hadn't I known that? How was I to know that this was where she felt safe, happy, at peace, that she was where she belonged?

Rejoicing, laughter, exclamations – all this I watched as if I were a total stranger watching two old friends reunite. Instantly, mother and daughter were catching up on family gossip and local happenings – if my older cousin was finally going to marry his girlfriend of three years, and how could an East German be named post-mistress? Of course, at that time, I did not understand a word of the conversation. Instead, I attempted to steel myself for three weeks of solitude in a country full of family. As my father unloaded the trunk, I turned around to rejoin my mother. I wanted to enter the house with her; I did not want her to be alone. But she wasn't alone. She wasn't even there. She had left me all alone. She could see me anytime, but she would see her family for only three weeks. Her brother, her sister, her many nieces and nephews, all waiting to see the youngest member of the Hansen family returned home. Realizing this, I walked through the doorway to endure unfamiliar greetings in an unfamiliar language in an unfamiliar place.

My displacement, in walking through the doorway,

was similar to my mother's displacement when she first came to America. I looked at all of the faces looking back at me, smiling, nodding, and asking questions. I constantly turned to my mother for a translation. I then answered in English, and she would translate my reply back into German. I felt both relieved and burdened. It was a relief to have someone close to me who could make sense of this foreign language. However, I felt like an encumbrance to the whole reunion. My mother flitted around the room talking to relatives she had not seen in three years. I followed her everywhere; I needed her to translate the essentials of the conversation to me. I could not go alone by myself – I could only communicate in smiles, shrugs, and nods.

My mother's displacement when arriving in America was similar. When she walked through the doorway of the household with my father for the first time, she knew none of the faces that looked and smiled at her. To her, each person was merely a member of her new husband's previous life. How was she to communicate with them? She stuck close to my father in talking with the family, but like me, she had trouble bridging the language gap. Although her English was considerably better than my German, she was not prepared for colloquialism or the accents that some of my father's relatives possessed. I was grateful that my mother was able to sift through the complex German that was thrown at me and provide me with something that I could understand – slang and accent-free German.

My mother's birthday arrived while we were still on vacation. I don't recall exactly who planned the party, but I do remember that none of the young children were invited. "Fine," I thought, "perfectly understandable. The adults just want time to themselves." However, on the day of the party, I did approach my mother to ask, "You will come by in the evening to say goodnight, right?" (To a twelve-year-old, these kinds of things are important.) "Yes, of course," she assured me, "You can count on it." With that in mind, the day proceeded smoothly. Later that night, I slowly got ready for bed – slowly, I knew, so that I could occupy myself while my mother made her way up the long staircase to my room I brushed my teeth, even flossed them. I washed my face, put on my night-gown, and I eased myself into bed and began to read…for an hour…and another. Tick, tock, the clock constantly reminded me. A knock. All of the angry thoughts drained out of me; I was merely relieved that she came, finally. But it was my father who pushed open the door. Even though I love my father deeply, I blurted out, "Where is she? Why doesn't she come?" My father knew of whom I spoke. "Vanessa," he said seriously as he sat down on the edge of the bed, "I don't think you understand the situation your mother's in right now. She hasn't seen her family in years. She misses Germany terribly. Can you imagine being separated from you mother and brother for three years, and living in a country where no on speaks your native tongue? Where the customs you followed as a child are not even heard of? How about living in this country against your will? I feel terrible that I was re-stationed in America. That's what your mother feels like a lot of the time. So let's allow her some fun while she's here. She's got a lot of catching up to do." And before I could say a world, he kissed me on the forehead and left the room.

About three days before we headed back, my mother took me by the arm and led me into the living room. "Come on, I want to show you something," she said. She saw my puzzled look and explained, "Let's look at some really old photos of my family." We started with the baby pictures. I saw an old black and white shot that showed three children – a five-year-old girl with brown hair stood behind a small block of wood, and a somewhat younger boy sat on the block of wood. "That's your aunt and uncle," my mother told me. "But who's that?" I asked, pointing to the blonde-haired baby who sat on the boy's lap. "That's me," she continued softly. We continued turning the pages. Was that really my Uncle Bernhard sitting on the tractor, holding my terrified mother when she was only five years old? Was that really my Aunt Friede helping my mother curl her hair for the dance? "Oh, oh," she would exclaim, "I remember that night. That was the night when our teacher took us out to our first beer hall. Oh, my, what a night that was...and there's my good friend...," and then I realized that at that moment, she was speaking only to herself. School events, family occasions, the departures of my aunt and uncle on their separate paths of life, the marriage of my mother and father; all these flew by us. For me, these pictures were new information, but for my mother they brought back precious memories. Occasionally, I would glance at her face, for she had grown quiet. Suddenly I understood why she stayed late at the party. I understood why she took long bicycle rides into the country. She wanted to store up wonderful memories, like those in the pictures, to last her until her next visit. This was a whole dimension of my mother that was just now coming to life – she had led a full, diverse life before my existence. It no longer hurt when I thought about the fact that she spent time in a whole different realm, an area of life of which I was simply not a part. So I understood why she cried when we came back. She had no idea when she would return to the house in which she grew up, to her family who knew her better than she knew herself, and to the land she found so beautiful.

Did I come closer to realizing that my mother was once like me? That she went out with friends? That she had arguments with her mother? That her siblings did things that she didn't tattle about? That providing milk and cookies for me is only a small part of her life? Yes. From that point on, I have looked at my mother in a whole new perspective. She is not only my mother, but a daughter, a sister, an aunt. And she has thoughts, hopes, and memories about a place which I may only visit and hope to learn about.

Works Cited

Friday, Nancy. *MY Mother/MY Self: The Daughter's Search for Identity.* New York: Delacorte Press, 1978.

The Lesson

Camille Whelan
Spring 1997 – Volume XVIII

My time in the Ukraine forced me to examine my advantages, which I had so taken for granted, and consequently, caused me to change my life philosophies. My Ukrainian experiences threw me into a blur of confusion about my priorities and goals. I was revolted. Most of all, though, I was exhilarated. Standing in the soggy streets of that city, I experienced a fleeting moment of understanding; a moment which was gone so swiftly it was almost incomprehensible, but which left me with the conviction that I was truly blessed.

Gabor, Vadim, Mr. Lareau, Rachel, and I arrived late at the Dudas's house in Vinogradov. From what I could surmise, the city was old-fashioned and glum; the houses, stone shanties surrounded by decrepit board fences. To my intrigued eyes, though, it was all mysterious and deliciously foreign. The barren countryside fascinated me, as did the woolen-clad families that tramped by, walking because they didn't have cars.

Shivering, I followed Mr. Lareau into one of the ramshackle yards. A scruffy dog, chained near the door, began to bark; and amid the clamor, the door was flung open and Rita Dudas and her sisters stood silhouetted in the warm light of indoors. Attracted by the hospitable light, I allowed myself to be drawn with Mr. Lareau into the girls' laughing, joyful midst. They immediately surround us, chattering excitedly and eying our American fineries with enchantment and wonder. Magdi, her soft brown eyes glowing, took our coats, while Rita consulted with Mr. Lareau in heavily-accented English and Kati watched us adoringly. Gabor, Vadim, and Rachel came piling in, and in the whirl of excitement that greeted their entrance, I took a moment to study my surroundings.

We were standing in a drafty cement entrance hallway. Cluttered with coats, boots, and stained furniture, it ended abruptly in a dingy bathroom. I could see into the next room, which was sparsely furnished with heavy wooden pieces. Garish colors screamed from every corner -rusty oranges pea greens, bawdy browns. Everything looked exhausted and ancient. I felt a surge of depression at what seemed a life of pathetic destitution. The girls were beckoning to me, though, smiling and chattering alternately in Hungarian and English, delightedly asking questions. I smiled in response, but their clothing horrified me, reminding me of cast-off 1970s attire. Their threadbare corduroy pants sagged off their hips, and foolish sweaters hung oddly from their thin shoulders. I jerked my eyes from the disturbing sight, disgusted by my snobbery. Their faces were so innocent and so ignorant of their ridiculousness that I cold not bear myself and my patrician thoughts. Was I really so decadent that I could attach such importance to the trivial matter of clothing. Was I so shallow that I could ignore the spiritual beauty that shone through their poverty? Resolutely, I buried my self-doubts, and allowed them to welcome me with kisses and seat me at the lavishly spread dinner table.

Dinner at least allowed me the opportunity to be silent and insignificant, since the Dudas's were very caught up with Mr. Lareau. Numbly, I gulped down a spicy concoction of noodles and slimy meat. Afraid to think about what I was eating, I concentrated instead on what was happening around me. Mr. Lareau, who commuted from Budapest to the Ukraine every weekend to conduct bible studies in Binogradov and the nearby city of Uszgorod, was chatting easily with the Dudas's. Mrs. Dudas in particular was fascinated by him and clung to his hands, drinking in his attention even though she understood him only through an interpreter. Puzzled by her eager responsiveness, I began to study discreetly the way she strove to fulfill his every whim, accepted his words without question or argument, worshipped him with her whole spirit shining in her eyes. It didn't occur to me until much later, after the Dudas's had retired and I was left alone to prepare for bed, that this woman's life was so simple the ministrations of a mere foreigner could bring her complete joy. To her, Mr. Lareau was a god – kind, gentle, omniscient, omnipotent. He was a hero. More than a little awed by this realization, I collected my soap and my face cloth and moved into the kitchen to wash my face.

As I huddled over the tiny kitchen sink, scrubbing my face, I reflected on the next day's schedule. Rachel and I would tour the marketplace and the downtown shops and then rendezvous with Mr. Lareau, Vadim, and Gabor in the main thoroughfare of Vinogradov. Mr. Lareau would then preach while Gabor and Vadim translated and Rachel, Magdi, Katil, Rita, and I would pass out tracts. I was avidly curious about the city: would it be as squalid as the Dudas's house seemed to be? Finishing with my face, I set down my bar of pineapple-oatmeal soap in the tray by the sink. I gazed for a moment at the rusty tray, then I saw the crumbling walls, the mildewed floorboards, and the meager, cracked dishes assembled beside the gnarled kitchen stove. The humble scene made my specialized soap seem terribly pretentious, and I was suddenly ashamed of my opulence.

It was with great reverence that Magdi awoke me the next morning. I smiled to indicate that no, I was not annoyed with her for disturbing me, and reassured, she beamed. After she was gone, a vague sense of trouble pervaded my mind. Was I, as a pampered, privileged American, really meritous of such worship? Trying not to feel silly at the excessive attention I knew my appearance would generate, I trudged into the kitchen to wash my face, and found Mrs. Dudas shredding cabbage.

"Jo reggelt," she chirped, and a painful conversation ensued, in which I struggled to understand her Hungarian and she, seeing my trouble, spoke even more loudly and with greater deliberation. Confused, I finally took to nodding my head whenever she spoke. In the midst of my consternation, I was struck by the fact that this visit, a fleeting moment in time for me, would be long cherished in their hearts. It seemed ironic that even though I had, since arriving, been continually reminded of the impact I was making on their lives, I was the one overwhelmed. I was the one being affected! And furthermore, here I was, caught in the trauma of two colliding worlds, incapable of even the most basic communication! The absurdity of the dilemma bordered on depressing. Luckily, I was rescued by the entrance of her husband, which distracted her enough to allow me, face still unwashed, to escape.

Rachel was awake and seated at the table when I sat down to breakfast. She looked mournfully up from the unappetizing contents of her plate, but continued eating without a word, since Rita was in the room. I gazed from the greasy slab of meat that lay on my plate to the oily black slosh in my coffee cup and thought with longing about the can of peaches in the travel bag I'd brought from Budapest. With no way to avoid eating breakfast and no explanation to justify myself to the Dudas's if I did, I rationalized that I was enriching my life with a cultural experience of which few could boast. Somehow, this conclusion made the tough meat seem more endurable.

Finishing breakfast quickly, we cleared away the dishes and then donned our coats to explore the marketplace. My spirits rose as I tramped along the avenue with Rachel and Rita. Both sides of the road were lined with magnificent cathedrals, and the passing natives on bicycles gave the scene a quaintness that appeased my battered sense of aesthetic appreciation, and almost atoned for the city's shabbiness. We passed a towering statue of Vladimir Lenin and I gazed in awe at the visage of this evil man who had kept whole nations groveling under Communism. My thoughts were occupied with socioeconomic structures as we entered the marketplace, so a moment passed before the scene registered with me.

A large, muddy lot sprawled before me, filled with frail, rotting booths. Cheap displays of eclectic Western paraphernalia abounded. Grimy gypsy children knelt in the muck, accusing the passers-by with silent, embittered black eyes. What arrested my attention, though, was a crowd of ragged peasants that surrounded a vegetable truck. A crew of men worked furiously aboard the truck, shoveling limp white roots into canvas sacks, and the air resounded with the squawks of the crowd as it jostled for attention.

I stared for a moment. These people were fighting for food – for mere roots! I was staggered. Never in my life had I conceived such poverty. I had heard since childhood, of course, about the sorrows of the people under Communism, but the harsh image of the oppressed masses, regurgitated in every political argument or commentary, had dulled into triteness. I was suddenly aware of how caught up I had been in myself and my painfully small world. Nothing anyone told me had prepared me for the decay and misery that I saw everywhere, in the neglected buildings, in the dreary marketplace and in the eyes of the careworn citizens I encountered in the streets. My disillusionment increased as sleet began to fall and cold drops lashed my face. I felt emotionally battered and wounded, and ashamed of myself, my country, and my wealth. I wanted only to crawl into a corner and cry. I struggled to keep my despair from showing, though, since I felt neither capable nor inclined to sharing my feelings with my companions.

As I stumbled miserably along after Rita, I thought about my life in America. As an American – prosperous, healthy, comfortable, secure – I had a great deal for which to be grateful. However, I had spent my life dwelling on my disadvantages. Born into a poor family, I had become accustomed to viewing myself as underprivileged and downtrodden, but now, confronted with real poverty, it occurred to me how ungrateful I had been. The thought stunned me. I had wasted the first half of my life wallowing in discontent, and it suddenly became very clear to me that I had no real reason to be discontented! Memories came flooding to me: memories of lavish Christmas dinners, of stockings stuffed with goodies, of my family's two cars, of my closet filled with colorful, eccentric shoes, of my sister's piano – small pleasures, really, that I had taken for granted. I had never had to fight in the mud for something to eat! It was indeed bewildering. I had never before considered my life beautiful and full and rich, but now I couldn't think of it as otherwise. The sleet was still slashing my face and cold was slowly numbing my body, but in that bleak moment, I felt absolutely and completely blessed.

Walt Whitman Was Wrong

Daniel Newell
Spring 1997 – Volume XVIII

Once I was bold and could speak with much more lit-erary creativity than this and go on and on about the same not-yet-dead topic for hours upon hours until finally I realized something. But I have become a coward, and will never quite express these truths to another human being except in the form of these jotted-down words. Ideas fester inside until I write about them or let them wither away into nothingness and get confused with all the other thoughts and emotions and fury and so many dreams. It is from this chaos that this idea comes, jumping out so brilliantly between my ears that I must free it in this medium out of fear that it will disappear like so many other thoughts. In other words, this is the story of the search of an unconfident, yet egotistical man, concerned with the world yet absent from it in all ways but that which is on the page.

Other people surround me but their faces are blank; their minds are a mystery, yet are the only things that matter for all, because those places are where the self is, they are where the essence lives, inside the mind and underneath all the meaningless appearances. Is this true self the being on the outside or is the true self that thing which exists on the other side of so many almost blank faces? So I guess what I am asking after all this stream of consciousness babble is: what is the essence of the worn-out-word "self"?

Does this self have its own identity, or is it so influenced by all the media and the images pouring in and the teaching and un-teaching and the religions and the demagogues and the sex and the drugs and flat out beat-ness that individualism is dead? Does the individual survive in the post 1980s world, where fringe is accepted, and being "different" is sold on the billboards and on the opium boxes in front of which we sit, submissively wasting our lives? In every big city or small town there is in every other apartment or home an anti-American dreamer who wants to be a filmmaker, artist, musician, actor, and dare I say writer. So many people these days want to be "different" or "special" that it would appear we are faced with the death of the individual. Is individualism dead? In order to decide if this is the case, an attempt must first be made to define an individual.

This is one of the oldest struggles that philosophers and poets alike have tried to tackle, and still few definitive conclusions have been reached. The young, as yet unpublished poet Tina Lawinski explored this in "The What You Are":

> But then he lets go too soon
> and leaves you standing naked in front
> of the mirror
> And the only thing you can possibly real-
> ize in the cold
> is that who you are,
> and the what you are
> And you want to throw the labels and
> limits and the
> definitions back in their faces
> for they had held you back all too long
> And you finally see

yes you finally see your own self
and you know
You don't need them anymore

Lawinski reached this conclusion for herself and that is all one can ask. However, no one else has to agree. The definition of an individual is and should be unique to each person who asks the question. So all I can attempt to do is form my own definition, being true to the chaos from which it comes, since it would be impossible and contradictory to attempt anything else.

The simplest place to start is with the basic definition that is attributed to the word "individual." A vast majority of those with whom I have discussed the topic define individual as being "different" from everyone else. "Different" meaning dressing, acting, and thinking in a way in which most other people do not. This definition is a good working explanation since it lays out some basic ground rules for being an individual. An individual must be in some way different from the norm. This idea would be perfect if we lived in a generation which has definite ideological norms and mainstream beliefs. In that case there could be a clear distinction between the masses and the individual.

Society has gone through periods where this is basically the case. In the 1950s there was a definite idea of the typical American(or at least that is how the story of the 1950s has come down in popular culture). Supposedly, in that time society was obsessed with the American dream, which is now a dead remnant of what it once was. This dream was the underlying social current of that generation. As we all know, it consisted of working hard, succeeding, raising a family, and keeping the cycle going. Of course, not everyone achieved this dream, but pop culture would have us believe that everyone strove to have a family with "two cats in the yard." We might have had to believe that everyone lived for this same purpose and that there was total conformity in the society at the time if not for a young boy named Holden Caulfield.

The Catcher in the Rye challenged the social norm of the day, the idea of the American dream. *Catcher* told the story of someone who dared to think differently. J.D. Salinger realized the meaninglessness of the prevailing social philosophy. Holden saw the phoniness apparent in a society that is conformist by nature. Throughout the novel, he uses the word "phoney" to describe anyone even remotely associated with the American dream. He drops out of school, and entire generations of people young and old still remember how they felt when they read of his adventures through New York for those few days. How his pure innocence, and his rejection of everything people ever thought he was inspired that rebellion inside. They remember how his love for his sister and contempt for his lawyer father made them want to run away and find some rye where they could catch those who are still real before falling into conformity. Those days where he was searching for something, something everyone should seek if there is to be such a thing as individuals, assuming that individualism ever matters.

Holden's world was so afraid of individuality that his search landed him in a mental hospital. This is not a testimony to what will happen if one goes on that search but what happens when not enough people do so. They are the ones who need help. If a society gets to the point where its members have no concept of themselves, the society is meaningless. Holden ending up in a psychiatric ward shows how crazy everyone else in that conformist society was, and how Holden was perhaps the only sane member of the whole group. His family and teachers feared his search and angst. They feared how real he was becoming, and how close he was to figuring himself out. Perhaps they were compelled to commit him because they were so out of touch with themselves that they could not understand Holden trying to find himself. The hospitalization shows the craziness of the world. Holden was not crazy, but unique, and it scared those around him. He was unique because he defied established beliefs and went on the all-important search.

Drawing from this, the next logical question that presents itself is: is individualism possible in a social era which has no established belief? *The Catcher in the Rye*, along with a plethora of other factors, caused the following decade to be one of anti-establishment. Everyone began going against the norms, and many young people were or at least attempted to be "different." There was no definitive belief system which could categorize the society in the age of protest. Or was there? That statement in itself, calling the '60s the "age of protest," is a statement of its beliefs. Even in a counterculture there are certain things in which a majority of the members believe. A group's beliefs may differ from larger parts of society's standards or social norms, but the members of the group are alike in the fact that they all disagree with some norm.

For example, the '90s is the so-called "alternative" era. Douglas Coupland's novel *Generation X* and the Rich Linklater film *Slacker* started a movement against society. Both told the story of disillusioned, unemployed youths who couldn't find meaning in the yuppified '80s world. Bands like Pearl Jam and Nirvana led a revolution in music and culture, proclaiming a non-conformist attitude and lifestyle. Those who follow this philosophy feel that they are "alternative," and against society. They are self-proclaimed rebels who don't want a cause. But this movement has become so popular that it constitutes a large portion of those under thirty years old. The society against which the movement went has ceased to exist. So they cannot all be alternative, since there is no longer anything to which to be alternative. The counterculture has been marketed and sold in the '90s, and now it seems like everyone is "alternative."

So the problem to which we have finally come is the concept that if everyone is different, everyone is still the same. The unity comes from the fact that many people believe in something, regardless of the essence of the idea. To illustrate this concept further, a large number of people disagreed with the Vietnam War. That made them different from those who supported the war but not from each other. So since there were many who disagreed with the same things, they cannot be called "different" in the sense that would make them individuals. So, still working in our original definition of "individual"(as one who is different from the rest), we can conclude that disagreeing with tradition or a mainstream part of society does not necessarily make one an individual. Individuals mean uniqueness, not just difference. It is possible for a group to be unlike the rest, but the simple fact that they are a group disqualifies them as individuals. If everyone is different, then everyone is the same.

And this is the problem with which my generation struggles. Individuality, in the traditional sense of the all-encompassing "different" theory (which has been shown to be a false definition) is the popular thing to be. No one wants to be like anyone else. The outsider is now the role model, the loser is now the saint. But this has become so prevalent an idea in the '90s that literally everything has been tried. There are no new ways to dress or act. Thinking is perhaps still free, but that is not really what it means to be an individual to "Generation X." It is the image of individuality that is sold to every youth.

Experimentation with sexuality and pseudo-spiri-tuality is everywhere. On every street corner there is an iconoclast standing on a soap box ready to scream at the next person who walks by. The downsizing of traditional jobs has fueled the movement towards art and music and film and so on. You never see an accountant or a teacher on MTV or "Entertainment Tonight." What used to be outside mainstream society has now been marketed and sold to us in so many mega malls. A *Time* magazine headline last year read: "If everyone is Hip...Is Anyone Hip?" Hip used to mean something underground and counter-culture and a hip person may have even fit the definition of "individual." The article pointed out that hip has totally lost this definition. Hip is now what everyone strives for. Whereas it used to be what people would avoid. The greatest irony is that the article was appear-ing in *Time* magazine. Such a huge enterprise as *Time* publishing an article on "hip" totally proves the point that hip and individualism are everywhere. They have become popular and consequently have lost their true meaning. If they still had their old essences, *Time* would never have considered running an article on them.

The same thing is happening all over the landscape of our national consciousness. The Gap put Jack Kerouac in an add for khaki pants. "Kerouac wore khakis" read the caption. The man must have rolled over in his grave. A capitalistic, corporate institution such as the Gap stands for everything Kerouac was against. The caption did not mention that Kerouac found most of his wardrobe in dumpsters and thrift shops, and that he could never afford Gap pants even if he wanted to wear them. While *The Catcher in the Rye* was being written (in the early '50s), Jack and his friends were driving back and forth across the country looking for the next new high or novel to write. *On the Road*, Kerouac's revolutionary novel, took free thought even further than *The Catcher in the Rye* did. Salinger's and Kerouac's ideas in the '50s became popular in the '60s and the decades after. The '90s are again an age of counterculture, and Kerouac's anti-establishment is again in fashion.

The *Time* article and Gap ad show that the idea of differences is the sought after status. However, obscurity does not necessarily equal uniqueness. So does this mean that the individual is dead? Yes, the traditional idea of individualism is dead, but the individual still survives. The fallacy lies in our old, used-up definition of an individual. The "different" individual is certainly dead. These days people try to be individuals not for the sake of finding their true selves, but because this is cool, hip, popular or whatever you want to call the things people strive to be.

So we must create a new definition of an individual, one that fits this complex time. We must attempt to come closer to its true meaning. This new definition must center around intent, not action or image. It must be rooted in the mind and the heart, not in the popular movements of society. Individuals are people who hold on to their beliefs, act how they act, and are who they are for themselves and themselves only. Not for popularity, not to go with or against anything, but simply because they are being true to themselves. Consequently, those who are different for the sake of being an "individual" are fooling themselves. Individuality lies in the following of one's soul, regardless if others call that person right or wrong or mainstream or different or any other limiting label.

This new definition centers on the self, on the inside. An individual can be like everyone else in style or thought or religion, as long as that person is honestly following him or her self. Two people could hold the same beliefs; let us say they both are pro-choice. If one has thoroughly thought through the issue and come to his or her own conclusion, he or she is making an individualistic choice. But if the other is simply pro-choice because he or she is following some political group or movement, then he or she holds a conformist belief. Following a crowd, even an extreme crowd, is still conformity and anti-individualism. Many ideas which differ from traditional norms are popular these days, such as homosexuality. So does that mean that no gay rights activists can be individuals?

Certainly not. The essence of individuality lies in the intent and the following of the self, so it is possible to go in the same direction as the crowd, yet not follow it. Consequently, one could take the most seemingly "conformist" person, someone pop culture would call a meaningless part of the masses, and if that person truly believes in everything that he or she does, no matter what anyone else has to say, then that person is a true individual. This new definition centers on the reason rather than the actual status or beliefs. If someone is an existentialist and holds that philosophy because it is in style, he or she is the farthest thing from an individual. But if another existentialist has read Sartre and Camus and truly believes in the philosophy, he or she can be called an individual.

In this age of counterculture and anti-American dreaming, the individual must let this idea of reason-oriented action permeate the entire philosophy of life. Everything, ranging from unimportant things such as style of dress to the most important things such as religion, must be deeply examined and contemplated. The search must take place on all fronts, but there is a catch. One must search for the self, not for the sake of being unique, because, as we have seen, this would be antithetical and would produce nothing but a pseudo-individual. One must search for the self because of one's burning need to find out who one really is. We need to cast off influences and up-bringings to become the people we are inside.

This search is what makes one a true individual if that even matters. Even if a million others are searching in an identical way, if their search is sincere, it creates an individual. Maybe you want to be an actor. Well, if you truly believe that acting is what is inside of you, then you are an individual. But what about a business person, not a job that carries the hip implication of "actor?" If you believe that a business person is what is inside, you are just as much an individual as anyone else. So what it all comes down to is following the heart and the dreams, regardless of the society around you. Everyone should take up this search, for if they don't, they will regret it their entire lives. Look at Prufrock.

The love song of J. Alfred Prufrock, by Thomas Stearns Eliot, tells of a desperate man tormented by his emotional paralysis in the face of his hope and dreams and ultimately his self:

> And indeed there will be time
> To wonder, "Do I dare," and "do I dare"
> Time to turn back and descend the stair.

Do I dare to find myself? Does the J. Alfred in everyone dare to search for the self? "Self-realization" is the best definition of individuality so far. Prufrock's lack of self realization causes his emotional impotence and identity crisis. It cause him to define himself as the most meaningless of creatures:

> I should have been a pair of ragged claws
> Scuttling across the floors of silent seas.

So according to Eliot, if one does not search for the self, all meaning will slowly drip away. If a person constantly does what others say, or always follows the crowd, that person will lose all ability to "move" under his or her own will. Man's soul will get lost in the crowd.

Take *Waiting for Godot,* the absurdist play by Samuel Beckett, that deals with the inability to act which comes from a lack of individuality. Two men stand by a tree waiting for someone named Godot who never comes. We do not know Godot. They never look for Godot, they never seek out Godot, and they never search for Godot. They suffer the same fate as Prufrock, an inability to act caused by a lack of self realization, a lack of individuality. The last lines of each act exemplify this idea:

Well, shall we go?
Yes, let us go.
Stage directions: *they do not move.*

If we do not seek out the self, inside, we will all end up perpetually waiting for Godot, and become a mass of conformists incapable of action. Never achieving individuality may not even matter, but never finding the self does. The search for the self must never stop. It is the most crucial part of being human, for if the self is never found, many Prufrocks will one day scream out at the same time, calling for the end of man. And if that day ever comes, there will be no way to find the lost time, to gather the rosebuds, and search for something real, something that matters, even for an instant, before Godot finally comes.

The search is not easy. It is a journey to a grand destination which is forever just beyond the next obstacle. It is always just barely in sight. Sometimes the end seems closer, other times it is far, far away. As one travels along this path, searching for that illusive self, one can laugh or cry or sing, and searchers usually do it all on a regular basis. Sometimes it is easy, other times it is hard. Finally, one may think that he or she has reached the emerald city, but once inside the gates, he or she finds a false wizard, or only a clue to where the real self is. This happens to many people when they really get interested in something, especially during their youth. How many young people play a musical instrument intensely for a few months and then lose interest? Different things appear to us to be our essences, and ourselves, but these things turn out to be nothing but petty imitations or answers that only create more questions. These questions make the never-ending search more difficult, and the journey more complicated.

And then there is that moment, that moment where you finally think you have reached the end of the journey, and have found the thing for which you were searching. The moment it occurs to you, out of nowhere, that you have found yourself, you are exhilarated and try to hold on to that moment for as long as possible, because you know without a doubt that it is real. You become an individual, and could care less about it, because that is not why you went on the journey in the first place. Then, as suddenly as it appeared, the moment is gone, and a thousand different new roads appear before your eyes, and the self that you just found needs to be sought after again.

This is the essence of an individual. Individuality is following hopes and dreams and loves, regardless of any outside influence or societies. It doesn't matter if a hundred or a million others are doing the same thing as you. If you are truly, not as Whitman said, "Marching to the beat of a different drummer," but marching to the beat of your own drummer, then you are an individual. And if being an individual is meaningless, at least you know what you are inside, and are still trying to find out more.

So all that is left to jot down is that the beat of your own drummer will beat away inside of you anyway, whether or not it is sought. So do not repress it as Prufrock did, and do not follow a false beat like so many others. Embark on the search for yourself and march to the beat of your own drummer. Time is not on your side. Don't end up at some nowhere stop just off the mainstream highway, and don't do things or believe ideas for the sake of being "different," or for any other popular trend. Follow your path until you find something real, until you reach that moment of truth, and then follow some more. What does your beat sound like? Do you even care?

Frightful Fun

Danielle Ariano

Spring 1997 – Volume XVIII

I present my fake ID to the bouncer at the door of The Bank in downtown Baltimore. He smiles, revealing his crooked teeth, and lets out a deep, quiet laugh from his bearded mouth. Running his fingers through his long, greasy hair, he eyes me. Abruptly, he shoves the ID back into my palm, and stamps my hand so solidly it throbs. I feel branded. I am ushered in the door by the people advancing in line behind me. Once I am inside, a large drop of some unidentifiable liquid splashes onto my head. Peering up at the ceiling, I cannot find its source. I notice a puddle at my feet, and realize that the drop I intercepted was intended for this small pool. I step out of the way, trying not to let it put a damper on my excitement for what the coming night holds.

I look around and see that before me lies a set of stairs to the lower level of the building. Curiosity about what is down there is interrupted by my friends. They are excited and sharing stories about the bouncer's reaction to their IDs. We climb three steps up to the large dance floor. The stage at the front is unoccupied. The band scheduled to play tonight is not going on until midnight, two hours away. We sit at one of the small tables that line the perimeter of the room. I scan the crowd, recognizing most of the faces as Loyola students, all sharply dressed. The far corner, where the bar is located, swarms with people eager for alcohol. I see a girl pushing her way fiercely through the crowd and coming out with a big smile and a beer, her barbarous behavior rewarded with the prized golden drink of choice. Those around her shoot her angry glances as she passes. On the remainder of the floor, groups of people gather to talk and dance as clouds of smoke curl above their heads.

The walls and floor of the room are painted black. The only lights are black lights that cast an eerie glow on anything white. I glance back at my friend and I am startled by the evil appearance of her eyes caused by the illumination of this strange light. When she turns her head she looks normal. Giant replicas of insects hang from the ceiling in attacking positions, creating a threatening atmosphere.

Since our arrival, a steady flow of people has been coming into the club, thickening the crowd each moment. We walk around to talk with everyone we know, and I nearly lose my friends twice as we make our way through the mob. With every step, I rub up against the sweaty body of some stranger, many of whom feel they have a right to grope my behind as I pass. We reach the other side of the room and stand in the corner. A boy with shaggy brown hair staggers by me and collapses into a nearby chair. Slumped over, he looks like a melted clay figure. He can't be any older than fourteen, yet he is obviously drunk, on the verge of passing out. This does not surprise me because most of the people in here are underage. His condition is horrifying, he is scarcely capable of holding his body upright, his hand hanging lifelessly between his legs. Some people stare at him with scared looks on their faces. I too am frightened, and approach him to see if he needs help. Squatting down to talk to him, I see that he is slobbering all over himself, and some of his saliva drips onto my jeans.

His words are barely comprehensible, but he tells me that he is okay, that he is here with his sister. The thought that he could die terrifies me, nevertheless, I slowly back away and leave the young boy slouching over in the chair. I try my best to put it out of my mind so that I can enjoy the night, but he remains impressed in my memory. As midnight approaches, there is a push towards the stage. When the band comes on, the crowd begins to dance. It surges to the rhythm of the music; bodies smash violently against one another. Because of their force, I can't help but to move with them. I am tossed from side to side, powerless and at the mercy of the unyielding group. I begin to wonder, is this supposed to be fun? The boy next to me in his impaired status appears to be having a good time, unaware of his disgusting surroundings. The rip in his expensive Ralph Lauren polo shirt and the couple beside him, who are about as close to having sex fully-clothed as you can get, don't seem to bother him in the least. In the midst of this bulldozing pack of people, a smile remains frozen on his face. In fact, most people here are so drunk they seem oblivious to the repulsiveness of this place. There is an unspoken rule that in order to have a good time you have to be drunk.

My friend taps me on the shoulder and I see her lips move, but I can't hear her above the blaring music. "WHAT!?" I scream back at her. She points to the stage with an inquisitive look on her face. I gather that she wants to go up to "dance." I hesitate, and then nod in agreement: I did come here to have fun. It seems that with every step towards the stage, we get shoved back to our original place, but finally we manage to make it. We engage in this form of hurling ourselves aimlessly around for five minutes before my friend gets elbowed in the ribs and knocked down. She has been permanently tattooed by boot marks and is covered by a dark, wet slime consisting of beer and whatever else might have been on the floor by the time she gets up. She and I depart from our group to head to the bathroom. The nearest ladies room is next to the stage. After pushing our way to it, we find that it is closed. The only other restrooms are downstairs, so we begin our journey across the room to the stairs. Halfway across the floor, a cup of beer is dumped on my head. I turn to see a girl standing with an empty cup and a shocked look on her face. She mumbles an apology and gestures to a guy wildly slam dancing next to her. My friend and I continue our battle towards the bathroom. Ten minutes later, we're downstairs. People are packed into two rooms. The smoke and heat are oppressive. It is a bit more quiet down here and I realize that my ears are ringing from the music upstairs. We find the bathroom. A line of girls extends out the door, and we place ourselves at the end. A girl sits next to the line, with her face buried in her knees. I've been there, alone and softly sobbing, just another nameless face in the crowd, another stranger no one cares about. I can see myself in her, and I remember how places like this can seem so fun until you find yourself separated from everyone. It is only then that you see the crowd for what it really is, a group of people linked by emptiness, searching for fulfillment in the bottom of a cup of beer. I pass her as we slowly advance in line. I can no longer remember why I came.

A foul smell hangs in the air and becomes stronger, more invasive, as we near the bathroom entrance. There are only two stalls inside, and one is occupied by a girl hugging the toilet. She sits besides a trail of her own vomit that leads into the bowl. Her friend is standing besides her holding her hair while she throws up. In the other stall, the seat is splattered with urine. A roll of toilet paper lies on the floor next to a used tampon. The walls are covered with obscenities. The cracked mirror hanging above the sink overflowing with cigarette butts reflects my image, slightly distorted, with a hot pink lip print stamped in the middle. As I stare at the mirror, I do not recognize my own filthy image. We abandon the ideas of cleaning ourselves up in the dingy room and return to the war zone above.

Back upstairs, the two of us decide that we have had enough of this place. We find our friends after a half hour search, and tell them that we are leaving. As I am walking to the door, another drop of mysterious liquid pelts me on my head. I am standing in the same puddle, which has now grown to twice its original size. I stare at it for a moment. It looks like a big, empty hole and it makes me think that weekend after weekend, month after month, this puddle forms in the same spot. I guess no one cares enough to find the source of the problem and fix it. When I finally step outside, I look down at the bottom of my jeans and shoes, both of which are caked with reminders of this hellish place. I don't know if I will ever get them clean.

The Evolution of Darkness

Josh Warner-Burke
Spring 1998 – Volume XIX

"This house is as dark as ignorance, though ignorance were as dark as hell," Shakespeare wrote in *Twelfth Night*. The word "dark" has traditionally been used to describe obscurity, ignorance, and evil. The connotation of darkness as obscurity is even present in the Bible: "Who is this that darkens counsel by words without knowledge?" (Job 38:2)[1] The tendency to use "dark" to describe obscurity is natural, as physical sight becomes limited in darkness, and the usage as ignorance seems to come from the age-old metaphor of knowledge as light. But how did dark come to mean evil?

Perhaps the connotation as evil comes from the human tendency to fear the unknown. Perhaps we fear what we cannot understand because we cannot control it. Certainly, wars have been undertaken because of a lack of understanding of another race, because of a desire to control it, and out of fear.

The fear of evil which darkness causes leads parents to demand their children be in by dark, and those children to cry at night for their parents to leave the light on. In general, we fear darkness, dark things, and the evil which lurks at night.

But in recent times, a subculture has slowly emerged which treats the word "dark" in a different way. It has in popular culture become an en vogue way to describe a new film or book or album; the word has evolved over time from meaning simply evil to meaning something much more complex, something good.

It is difficult to determine when the change began to occur, but the roots of the change can perhaps be traced to the Gothic novels and short stories of the 18th and 19th centuries. The Gothic tale presented darkness as a means of inspiring fear in its audience, and this was its primary appeal. As Chris Baldick explains in the introduction to *The Oxford Book of Gothic Tales,* "It is customary to account for the appeal of Gothic fiction by reference to a set of universal and timeless dreads usually referred to as 'our deepest fears'."[2] The dark aspect, although meant to be frightening, was the key element of the fiction of the time and likely what made the readers keep coming back.

That Gothic tales were inherently dark and dreary can be seen even in the first sentence of Edgar Allen Poe's classic "The Fall of the House of Usher":

> During the whole of a dull, dark, and soundless day in the autumn of the year, when the clouds hung oppressively low in the heavens, I had been passing alone, on horseback, through a singularly dreary tract of the country; and at length found myself, as the shades of the evening drew on, within view of the melancholy House of Usher.

That people kept coming back to this dark world is significant. They must have been drawn to it. As Rudolph Otto described the fascination he described the device which made Poe and other Gothic writers so popular:

The daemonic-divine object may appear to the mind an object of horror and dread, but at the same time it is no less something that allures with a potent charm, and the creature, who trembles before it ... has always the impulse to turn to it, nay even to make it somehow his own. The 'mystery' is for him not merely something to be wondered at but something that entrances him ... he feels a something that captivates and transports him with a strange ravishment, rising often enough to the pitch of dizzy intoxication; it is the Dionysiac element in the numen.[3]

Then in the 19th century darkness was used by the Symbolist Movement in art. As Robert Goldwater writes, "Symbolists and thought-painters alike wanted to give pictorial form to the invisible world of the Psyche."[4] The paintings, such as Franz Von Stuck's *Sin,* use darkness strategically to engage the imagination, and they also portray "dark" desires. Freudian psychologists would suggest that they satisfy the "id" which lurks in the darkness of the unconscious and helps to propel the conscious mind.

Silence by Odilon Redon is often cited as the epitome of Symbolist style and intent. Goldwater explains the essence of dark art in that *Silence* "contains that suggestion of the mysterious reality beyond appearance ... both in its subject, which stresses a concentration upon the usually unseen and unheard, and in its handling, which suggests more than it depicts."[5] In essence, dark art stimulates the unconscious mind to fill in the shadows.

Redon wrote to his Dutch patron Andre Borger, "My sole aim is to instill in the spectator, by means of unexpected allurements, all of the evocations and fascination of the unknown on the boundaries of thought."[6] When one looks at a painting such as *My Irony Exceeds All Others* there is not much to see at first; the painting is difficult to grasp as it is mostly black, but there is much more to the painting than what one can first see. One must let one's unconscious mind fill in the black space for it to become a whole painting.

Darkness, the absence of light, is similar to silence, the absence of sound. Silence, Goldwater writes, "was of course not merely the simple absence of sound, nor was it an end in itself: one cultivated silence as a means of shutting out appearances in order to concentrate upon essence, and so isolation became the condition through which the artist could ignore the material and thus be able to penetrate the spiritual."[7] Perhaps darkness was appealing to the Symbolists for the same reason – the concentration upon the spiritual.

Joseph Conrad is said to have drawn upon both the Symbolist ideas and the Gothic form in his dark novels, especially *Heart of Darkness*. There have been countless interpretations of *Heart of Darkness* because Conrad meant to obscure its meaning. Allen White, in *The Uses of Obscurity,* says that Conrad's fiction "deploys a variety of figures which combine to imply that the narrative is only a hint or a clue to some immense secret enclosed within it. The tragic gloom which hangs listlessly over so many of the stories can be related both to the threatening proximity of this transcendent symbolic realm, and to the lack of any possibility of locating it." The entire novel is about Marlow's journey up river into the "heart of darkness" – that is, obscurity. There is almost nothing in the novel which is described concretely; everything is "impenetrable" or "inscrutable"; Conrad doesn't want us to grasp hold of anything in his story tightly, and he means to tell us nothing concretely except perhaps that life is, for the most part, unknowable.

White goes on to explain that the inscrutable nature of Conrad's fiction also serves as a mirror of the reader. "Proust has remarked that 'Some people who are fond of secrets flatter themselves that objects retain something of the gaze that has rested upon them.' This enigmatic flattery operates like Borges' story *The Mirror of Enigmas* in that it makes the enigmatic endlessly reflective (in both senses of the word). The transference from subject to object, inverting the relation of questioned and question … is an essential part of the structure of *Heart of Darkness*"[8] and this reflectiveness echoes the aim of the Symbolist painters.

Darkness became important again in the 1930s and 1940s in comic books and the pulp fiction of crime novels. The dark aspect had at that time become the violence with which heroes and villains alike battled each other. Freud's theory stated that most of human motivation involves sex and violence, and the crime novels and comic strips beginning in the '30s had much to do with both. For example, the *Dick Tracy* comic strip by Harold Gould was violent and what would be described as dark. In comics like *Dick Tracy* the villains were perhaps more notable than the detectives. Wiley Lee Umphlett, in *Mythmakers of the American Dream*, suggests that the reason why such crime drama was so popular is that we feel a nostalgia for violence – "a recognition of some forgotten emotional experience from our distant past through re-experiencing a graphically visualized portrayal of man's inhumanity to man."[9] That sex was a large part of these crime novels can be easily seen on any *Mystery Adventure* cover.

The most influential example of deliberately dark art is the film noir of the '40s. As *The Oxford Companion to Film* explains, "German filmmakers pioneered a form of horror film (such as *Nosferatu* in 1922) using oblique lighting and compositional tension rather than physical action to create a nightmare world of violence... and these elements were fed into the Hollywood gangster tradition by the German directors and cameramen who went to the U.S." [10]

The *Maltese Falcon* with Humphrey Bogart is a prime example of film noir, and much can be learned from its technique as to why such a dark movie would have such appeal to a large audience. A central characteristic of such film noir is the incompleteness of perception. In an early scene Sam Spade (Bogart) gets a call, and during the call Spade is off screen, and the voice on the other end is not heard. The viewer is not told what is going on but has to guess, much as one has to feel one's way around and draw conclusions when walking in the dark.

The oblique lighting derived from German films causes every man to have a shadow, which acts as a symbol of the dark side of his personality. These shadows, these dark sides, are noticeable throughout the movie. The characters, then, are acting on their dark desires. And the viewer wants that – the viewer wants to see the "corrupt" – perhaps to look down upon it but more likely to live vicariously through it.

Before Sam Spade gets to know his fellow star, Bridget O'Shaughnessy (played by Mary Astor), the following dialogue takes place:

> Sam: You aren't exactly the sort of person you tend to be, are you?
> …
> Bridget: I haven't lived a good life; I've been bad. Worse than you would know.
> Sam: Well, that's good, because if you actually were as innocent as you pretend

to be, we'd never get anywhere.
Bridget: I won't be innocent.
<u>Sam:</u> Good.

And in that, he describes the dark aspect of film noir: we want the characters to break the rules and be "bad." But there's more which film noir added to the concept of darkness.

At the end of the movie Sam is not persuaded by Bridget to go with her. He says he might love her, but he turns her in to the police because he knows he could never trust her because she killed his partner, "and it's not good for business if you know who killed your partner but they don't get it in the end." Essentially, he rejects sentimentality and caring, and he champions honor, machismo, and autonomy. With film noir, darkness in art became also the rejection of altruism and the embrace of an "every man for himself" philosophy. Viewers could, for the two hours of a film noir, be selfish, and live out another dark desire.

In the 1960s even music began to become dark. Jim Morrison and The Doors reached immense popularity singing and talking about dark desires. In Jim Morrison's *An American Prayer,* an album consisting of music and poetry intertwined, he talks about places where the human spirit is left on its own to do as it pleases:

> My gang will get you.
> Scenes of rape in the arroyo.
> Seductions in cars, abandoned buildings.
> Fights at the food stand.
> The dust.
> The shoes.
> Open shirts and raised collars.
> Bright sculptured hair. [11]

Also to be noted is the music which accompanies the preceding lyrics; the music is playful and rhythmic. The words and music describe a free, happy place. In short, the song indulges a fantasy of anarchy and indulges dark desires.

He also liked to sing and talk about despair and searching in darkness for something essentially human. The night and the moon show up frequently in his poetry and music. An example can be seen again in *An American Prayer:*

> Let me tell you about heartache and the loss of god,
> Wandering, wandering in hopeless night.
> Out here in the perimeter there are no stars,
> Out here we is stoned
> Immaculate. [12]

The "wandering in hopeless night" reminds one of the incompleteness of perception involved in film noir. Morrison sang the poetry of confusion. He sang about basic human feelings and desires, such as sex, violence, sadness, and the search (in darkness) for a higher purpose. In Morrison's music, darkness and night are used in much the same way as Conrad's *Heart of Darkness* – to emphasize the final impenetrability of things.

Today in the 1990s dark art has reached a high point and has achieved mainstream popularity. One can hear it in popular music and see it in the theaters; there is a huge market for dark art. Take, for instance, some lyrics from Metallica, a heavy metal band whose "Black" Album (it is a self-titled album whose case is all black) has sold 15 million copies:

Something's wrong, shut the light
Heavy thoughts tonight
And they aren't of Snow White

Dream of war, dreams of liars
Dreams of dragon's fire
And of things that will bite

Sleep with one eye open
Gripping your pillow tight[13]

In movies especially, the dark has become a symbol much striven for. Could Quentin Tarantino have sold a movie ten or twenty years ago? *Reservoir Dogs, Pulp Fiction,* and *From Dusk Till Dawn* have all achieved a great deal of success in spite of the fact that they are graphically violent and focus on the adventures of violent criminals; once again one could easily conclude that they have been successful because of their violent nature. In the '90s we have embraced the antihero: The Joker in *Batman,* Brandon Lee in *The Crow,* and Vincent Vega in *Pulp Fiction* are only a few examples.

Escape From L.A. by John Carpenter, a sequel to *Escape From New York,* is the epitome of dark art as it has come to be defined. Snake Plissken, played by Kurt Russell, is essentially a cowboy stuck in a society which has exiled everyone who does not conform to the lofty morals set forth by its dictatorial ruler. He is a misfit, and we love him for it. He dresses in black leather and packs more than one gun. He smokes in a society which does not tolerate it. He lives out the secret desires of a large part of a generation; he gets the women, cares only about himself, and does anything to get ahead. We love his immorality, just as Sam loved Bridget's in *The Maltese Falcon.*

The movie comes to a climax when Snake gets hold of the remote controlling an Electromagnetic Pulse weapon in outer space with the power to destroy every electric circuit in the world. He holds the remote, and the president of the United States begs him not to use it: "You'll destroy everything we've worked so hard for," he urges.

Snake looks around and we know he sees nothing worth keeping. He punches in the code, 666, and the satellite shuts everything down. The world goes black. Symbolic night has been achieved. He walks away from his captors, their weapons useless. He finds a pack of cigarettes and coolly lights one up. He takes a drag, looks at the camera, and says, "Welcome to civilization." Fade to black.

> I feel a change
> Back to a better day
> Hair stands on the back of my neck
> In wildness is the preservation of the world,[14]

Metallica wrote in "Of Wolf and Man". Dark art has become a release for our deepest desires for violence, sex, and anarchy. It is a way for us to live out those desires vicariously and nondestructively. It is a way for us to get in touch with our primal selves, and experience the nostalgia for a forgotten emotional experience in our distant past that Umphlett describes. Darkness is something we no longer fear.

Works Cited

[1] *The Oxford Annotated Bible* (New York: Oxford University Press, 1977).

[2] *The Oxford Book of Gothic Tales,* Chris Baldick, ed. (New York: Oxford University Press, 1992), 11.

[3] Rudolph Otto, *The Idea of the Holy: An Inquiry into the Non-Rationed Factor in the Idea of the Divine and its Relation to the Rational,* trans. John W. Harvey (New York: Oxford University Press, 1924), p. 31, as quoted by David R. Saliba, *A Psychology of Fear* (Washington, D.C.: University Press of America, 1980), 3.

[4] Robert Goldwater, *Symbolism* (New York: Harper and Row, 1979), 9.

[5] Ibid., 26.

[6] Ibid., 116.

[7] Ibid., 120.

[8] Allen White, *The Uses of Obscurity* (Boston: Routledge & Kegan Paul Ltd., 1981).

[9] Wiley Lee Umphlett, *Mythmakers of the American Dream* (Cranbury, NJ: Cornwall Books), 92.

[10] *The Oxford Companion to Film,* Liz-Anne Bawden, ed. (New York: Oxford University Books), 249.

[11] Jim Morrison, "Black Polished Chrome" from *An American Prayer* (Elektra Entertainment Group, 1995).

[12] Jim Morrison, "Stoned Immaculate" from *An American Prayer.*

[13] Metallica, "Enter Sandman" from *Metallica* (Creeping Death Music, 1991).

[14] Metallica, "Of Wolf and Man" from *Metallica.*

Easter 1996

Alison Esposito
Spring 1998 – Volume XIX

I am not traditionally religious, but I know the stories. Christ was crucified on Good Friday, and three days later, on what we now call Easter Sunday, Christ rose from the dead and appeared as a sign of hope for all the peoples of the world. It is with searing irony that on the exact day of Christ's resurrection, one thousand, nine hundred and ninety-six years later, one believer was robbed of all the hope she had ever known.

I was born the fifth day of January in the Year of Our Lord, 1978. On this day, the chill outdoors was comparable only to the freeze of the ninth circle of Dante's Inferno.[1] This state of weather is related to me each year at my birthday dinner by two of my uncles who are in attendance, after which my mother annually remarks that it was the best day of her life, and my father remembers being overjoyed simply because I was "normal." These dinners proceeded in exactly the same fashion every year: routine, but happy – one big happy family of which my mother and father were the pillars upon which everyone else, myself included, leaned. We were a strong family, and since I was their only child I received all of my parents' attention. Actually, all of my mother's attention, for my father's thoughts were always devoted to work – a survival mechanism for him which I could not understand. My father rose every day at four or five o'clock in the morning, and I rarely got to see him, save those infrequent occasions when he wouldn't leave until six o'clock. On those days I would wave to him through the cold glass of the front door as he honked the horn of his immense, steel truck and made the sign language sign for "I love you" with his hand. These deaf moments were the closest we ever came to communication.

When I was very young, I often refused to speak to my father when he came home; I would not give him a hug when he returned from the darkness outside at eight or nine at night, because he never really returned from the dark space in my mind. I saw him as a distant identity – far-removed from my world, but not really having one of his own; the sad part was that I knew he wanted to be a part of my life, but I could not let him. Every night that he was home for dinner he would ask me what I had done that day, and each evening I would reply "nothing," unable to relate to him any of the day's events which fifteen or twenty minutes ago I had just told my mother with such enthusiasm. The "A" on the paper seemed unimportant, my running time was not so special after all, and the gossip – well, he could never remember the names of my friends anyway – it would be a waste of time to try to explain it to him. So each night my father was home for dinner, when he asked me what I had done that day, my mother would reply enthusiastically, informing him of my "wonderful" grades, my fast times, my life. It was through her that he knew me, and that I gained my limited knowledge of him. My mother not only supported but built the relationship that I had with my father. The issue was not that I hated him, it was that I never knew him, and the rift between us only grew greater as the years went on.

My mother and I, on the other hand, grew closer with the passage of time. She, always home and ever-ready to help me whenever I needed it, became my closest friend.

She was reliable, always wanting to hear my problems and always having an answer. When I was small, my mother stayed home with me. In elementary school, she took me to the school bus, and in middle and high school, she drove me to and from school until I was old enough to drive. She packed my lunches through the twelfth grade. Ironically, as I grew older and more independent, she became a bigger part of my life, but not so much as a mother anymore – as a friend. This is not to imply that we got along all the time, because we definitely did not, but we never really had fights – the screaming sort that we both had with my father.

My father often proved to be a source of anger for both my mother and me, but while she could deal with him on an adult level, I was powerless against his fits of irrationality. So my mother would work things out between us when we would argue, and she would try to explain to me that my father loved me and would do absolutely anything for me, if only I asked him. I never asked him. I guess I could not believe her, and I knew I could not talk to him. I was sure, though, that my mother loved me and would do anything I asked of her. She knew everything about me, and I thought that I knew everything about her. Trusting one person so much was the most costly mistake that I have ever made in my life.

Trust, you see, is a false friend. It blinds you to reality, makes you feel emotions unconditionally, and it is like a pillar, for if you lean on it too hard and too long it is bound to give way. And when it does, it is as though the Coliseum has crumbled down upon you. I trusted my mother infinitely, so I never saw it coming until one day, all of a sudden, the Coliseum fell down on me and crushed my soul. So it happened that on the day upon which Christ rose from the dead, one thousand, nine hundred and ninety-six years later, my mother delivered to me the news of her own resurrection, leaving me to take her place hanging on the cross.

"No I will not come and live with you, are you crazy?" My mother actually expected me to move out of the house in which I had lived for eighteen years and into a townhouse with her and her new boyfriend. In doing this, I would be leaving my father to fend for himself, completely alone in the country just six months before I was to leave for college. "You don't understand." "It's not your fault." "It's not you I'm leaving, it's your father." I had made an attempt to keep the anger from oozing through the pores of my skin, but it was not working, for my mother continued to backpedal. I was also trying to keep my sarcasm in check, but it was getting harder with every word that came out of my mouth attempting to explain why she was leaving my father after twenty-one years of marriage, and for a man that she had been having an affair with for just months. Funny, I thought adultery was a sin – so why was I the one with a stake through my heel, being hauled up to hang from my outstretched arms? Completely defenseless, I began to see everything in a new light, through eyes rolled back and tinted red with blood.

My vision impaired, I almost did not see that she had left two weeks later. The day she moved her things out of the house I was not at home, so nearly everything was the same as usual when I returned from school that evening. There were a few books missing from the bookshelves, some paintings were gone, and one closet was now empty in my parents' bedroom, but other than that nothing had changed. It was hard to believe that all my mother amounted to was some books and clothes, but that was how it seemed, and it wasn't as if anything was really gone.

Not gone for very long at least, for, you see, my

mother was coming back. She had a momentary lapse of reason, but she would soon return to her senses and to our house and make it whole again. Every day I heard this reassurance from the voice in my mind, but every day this voice became a little more hoarse, a little more tired, until finally it fell silent, unable to utter another word.

The silence at the dinner table was, at first, stifling. Because my father and I had never had to directly communicate with each other, it was an awkward endeavor. Neither wanted to talk about what had happened, but we really didn't know much about each other's lives, so the topic of conversation each night rested on what we had done that day. I could understand little of (and cared less about) what my father had done with his truck's transmission, and preferred to reside in my mind's silence rather than make the Herculean effort of explaining to him what was going on in my life.

As I had done as a child, I kept him and his world far removed from me and mine. He tried to break through the icy wall that I had built up against him over the years, but he had little success, for no matter how hard he tried, this wall could not be broken. It had to melt, and in order to do that my heart had to be warmed. Three months, five months, seven – and my heart was as cold and stony as ever, for I thought that I needed no one's help, no one's friendship, no one's love. After all, if my mother had stopped loving me and I had not died in the process, surely love was not something that I needed in order to live. I would simply live without it, then; the issue was decided – but things just kept getting more and more confusing, more and more difficult, more and more frustrating, and every day I got more and more angry until one day the ice around me cracked under the pressure. The split slit through the hard ice, through my thick skin, and I bled. The shocking sight of the red stream flowing from my body frightened my heart back to life and back to warmth, just enough to begin to melt the wall around me. Although I slid, and sometimes fell, climbing over the slippery, watery red mess melting around me, I grabbed hold of my father's hand and came to stand on solid ground. And I began to see my father in a different light.

Since then I have come to realize that my father and I are not so different at all, our worlds are not so separate as I once thought them to be. In fact, I see a lot of him – his actions, his thoughts, his mannerisms – in me, and I have begun to trust him, to tell him my problems, and to learn from his advice rather than tune it out. He knows much, much more about life than I ever realized. He is one of the kindest men I know. He is a great friend. He has become what I always thought a father should be. Most of all, though, my father succeeds (and this is no easy task) in giving me hope for the future, in making me see that I can trust again, and in letting me know that love is not always as fickle as it seemed to me almost a year ago. And he is managing, slowly, to pry free from my blood-stained hands and feet, the nails of disillusionment with which my mother crucified me, so that I may move on to a better world.

Notes

[1] The ninth circle of Dante's Inferno is the level of Hell where those whose sin is betrayal of family are punished: it is a frozen-over lake which holds the unmoving bodies of the sinners.

The Afterglow in Bayonne

Lee Abbey
Spring 1998 – Volume XIX

We walked along the city streets. It was nighttime and it was winter and we could see our breath in front of us. Main Street was deserted. The sidewalks were cold, or warm from neon lights that hung gently buzzing blue and red in the windows of closed-up stores and second-rate bars. We floated by these lights, bathed in fluorescent glowing shadows, and we talked about how good it was to be dead. We walked alone, in no particular direction, ignoring the crosswalk signals that flickered orders at people who were already tucked away in their apartments and at cars turning cold in their garages. It was a wonderful time to be a ghost in Bayonne.

"If you had to choose between being rich and unhappy or poor and completely happy with your life, which would you choose?" I asked.

He said, "I'd much rather have the money. In my experience I've found that money can equal happiness."

"You capitalist pig."

"And you, my friend, are a communist who'll never know how it feels to climb the social ladder all the way to, to, to – "

"To what?"

"I don't know. But I'll make sure I write you a postcard from wherever it is."

Life was very simple when we were dead and talking in Bayonne. Neither of us ever heard an argument from a street light or a sewer, only friendly echoes from the alleys between sets of brownstone buildings and bakery shops with unsold bread going stale on deserted shelves. I thought of businesses like that: not a way of satisfying a basic human need, but an empty stomach, a stomach that starved for the hunger of others. I looked at my friend, my only friend at the time, and then I looked at the sleeping shops with their doors locked tight and their dreamy reflections in the windows. And I decided to keep my mouth closed – I didn't want to let anything go stale.

In Bayonne there is a park where you can sit on benches and look out at the Bayonne Bridge. The view would be unbearable during the day, with the sun and its detecting rays seeking out the dealers, the decadence and garbage tossed from car windows and frozen on the grass. But the night was kinder to ghosts in Bayonne. All signs of life would sleep under its blanket and our eyes could relax enough to see that what is bearable becomes beautiful when you're a ghost in Bayonne.

"Did you know Ginsberg mentioned this bridge in one of his poems? Here, take one of these."

"What is it?" I asked.

"I don't know, some kind of painkiller. I stole it from my mom's purse."

"Well, what does it do?"

"It kills pain, you idiot."

"I'm just afraid it might kill me, you know?"

"Take a look around, Chief. We're already dead."

On the park bench we found ourselves surrounded by the numbing chill of winter, broken from time to time by the sounds of the river water splashing against artificial banks. We felt privileged to sit in this temporary half-heaven with nothing around that could possibly haunt a ghost. Except, maybe, the promise of day.

"Do you remember a movie called *Heaven is a Playground*?" I asked him.

"Yeah, we'd pick it up and read the cover but never rented it. God, what a concept – 'heaven is a playground.' What do you think that makes hell?"

"Hell, I guess, is where all those children stand, outside the fence, looking in and watching the others play."

I looked around. "Do you think anyone is watching us?"

"I doubt it. Everyone's asleep."

We got up from the bench and began walking again, this time towards his house so we could escape the rising sun. We walked along the sidewalks. It was still cold but the darkness was starting to fade. Step on the cracks, break your mother's back, step on the cracks…

I don't think we missed a single one.

He said, "It's not that I don't like her. I just seem to feel better when she's not around."

"I once wrote a story about a kid who just couldn't bear to say goodbye to his mom in the morning, so what he did was stuff her into an oversized book bag and carry her wherever he went. All was going well. He learned to just ignore his mother's muffled cries for help until, one day, he began to feel hungry because he didn't know how to cook. He tried asking his mother for instructions but he couldn't make out her exact words. So he had to choose between starvation and the chance that his mother might get away from him."

"So what happened?" my friend asked.

"So he finally decided to open the bag. But, you see, his mother was stuffed in so tightly that when the zipper opened it snipped her jugular vein and she bled to death. The kid died, too, from the shock of seeing his precious mother lying there, and fell on top of her, a lifeless heap of unconditional love. It was all very tragic."

My friend paused. "What the hell is the point of that?"

I answered, "I have no idea."

After a while, my friend said, "That could never happen with my mother. I think our relationship is too open for that sort of extreme affection."

This was true. There on the sidewalks we found ourselves laughing as the dawn crept up behind us – it was getting lighter with every step. Soon we would be required to live, to share thoughts with the thoughtless, to fight with strangers for the back seats of cabs, and to read the news in black and white with tired eyes...

It was all very tragic.

Shoot for the One in the Middle

Katherine Repetti
Spring 1998 – Volume XIX

Only twenty-five seconds remaining, and we were still down by two points. The high-pitched squeal of the whistle echoed through the enormous gymnasium. "Time out," my coach yelled. We all hustled to the sidelines, and smacked our butts down upon the splintered, wooden bleachers. "All right," he said, rather frazzled. "Megan, you bring the ball down, and pass it out wide to Katherine. Katherine, you just be sure to get the ball in to Debs." He turned toward Debbie and simply said, "Do your stuff, kid." The buzzer called us out to the court once again. This play was nothing special, but it would work. As long as we got the ball to Debs, our fate would be sealed. Debs, who was often referred to as "Diesel," could break through anyone to get the ball into the bright orange rim.

The whistle blew and it all began. Megan quickly got the ball down the court, and into my hands. As Debs flashed across the court, I chucked the ball her way. She caught it, and, with three players guarding her, went up strong and shot the ball. It bounced off the backboard and through the net. While our eyes watched, our ears were disturbed by the sound of one final whistle. "Foul!" the ref exclaimed. We all danced with joy! Debs would get to shoot one foul shot. If she made it, the victory would be ours.

She positioned herself at the line. I made my way over and slapped her hand. "Repets," she whispered, "What do you think, shoot for the one in the middle?" I just laughed. Throughout the season, Debs had had this triple vision problem. Between school and practice, she hadn't found the time to get a new and improved set of contacts. It was a common joke among us. Always shoot for the middle we had both agreed at the beginning of the season.

Finally, the ref tossed her the ball. "One," he said firmly. She bounced the ball twice, positioned it comfortably in her hands, and released it. Floating freely through the air, it successfully reached its destination. We had won! I ran and jumped on Debs, followed by the rest of the team.

Just a few weeks later our season ended, and we returned to the regular school routine. I walked into study hall and looked for Debs. Suddenly, I remembered that she was absent because she was finally making the trek to the eye doctor. That evening I heard my phone ring and raced upstairs to get it. I answered, breathing heavily from my strenuous dash, and heard nothing but complete silence. I was going to hang up when I heard a mumbled, "Hey Repets." "Hey," I replied. This was not the usual "Hey Repets," that I received around nine o'clock every night. Something was wrong. She didn't call to talk about school, guys, or to just joke around; no, it was nothing like that. She had called to tell me something terrible, to ramble off a line that I would remember for the rest of my life. "Repets," she managed to squeak, "I'm at New York University Medical Center. I have a brain tumor." Shocked, I said nothing. I didn't know what to say. Even if I did, my throat would never have softened enough to allow me to reply. Then all I heard was a click; she had hung up.

I just sat paralyzed. I was devastated. What did this mean? So many thoughts raced through my head. Was she going to die? What if this tumor was cancerous? Was this mass the cause of her triple vision that we had joked about so frequently? Emotions overwhelmed me. I was angry, confused, and upset all at once. I could not imagine my life without my best friend by my side playing basketball, discussing everyday gossip, sharing our wild and magical dreams, and just being best friends. What would life be like?

Further tests proved the worst. The doctors claimed that the tumor growing behind her right eye was malignant. My best friend, only seventeen years old, was suffering from cancer. This had to be a mistake.

The entire summer, Debs underwent chemotherapy and radiation treatment with the hope that she would conquer her disease. Many times these treatments made her incredibly ill, but other times she was healthy enough to continue a slightly altered version of her normal, teenage life.

Each time I visited her, I could see her decaying physically. She lost a lot of weight, she lost all of her hair, and the skin on her head, neck and chest was charred a dark, brownish-black form the radiation. Debs always thought that she would recover, and never let anyone tell her differently. She was determined to use all her strength to pull through and defeat her disease, just as she used her strength to score the winning basket, and defeat our rivals. It was this positive attitude, and her love for life that kept her going strong.

Out of nowhere, toward the end of the summer, her regular MRIs showed that the tumor was shrinking! She started to get better! The treatments were working! A miracle! She would be okay; things would return to normal! Debs continued her treatment faithfully, even though the cure was making her very weak and at times violently ill. She was going to beat the disease that she was contending for her life.

The doctors were amazed at how well she was responding. But, the rigorous treatments soon became too much for her rundown body to handle. She could no longer remain healthy through the treatments; she contracted pneumonia. The treatments had to stop. Each test verified that the tumor was once again growing.

From this point on, Deb's health declined rapidly. Her once strong, and shapely body was now bony and pale. She could no longer walk, or even sit up on her own. Her triple vision turned into a single, dark, blurry picture. She was completely helpless, and had to rely on everyone else to help her live what life she had left in her. I'll never forget the day that I went to visit and she did not know who I was. I tried so hard to understand, but it hurt so much. For the first time, I was forced to face the fact that my best friend was going to die. I did not want to scar my memory of her any further. This was not the Debbie that I wanted to remember. This was not my Debbie.

A week went by. I had not even called to see how she was, even though I longed to find out her status. I knew that she was dying, and all that I could do was wait for that one phone call – the call that would be the most devastating, yet the most relieving. Each time the phone rang, I could not help but think that maybe this was the call that would inform me that she was gone.

Suddenly, I changed my mind. I was in school and I decided that I must see her. I don't know where the sudden impulse came from. It was like a little voice was telling me that her time was almost up. I left school and drove in a frenzy to her house. I talked to her mom for over two hours. Together we sat and conversed, all about Debbie. She showed me numerous pictures of her, and we exchanged countless stories of our own experiences with her. I saw pictures of her as a precious ballerina, a graceful side of Debs that I never knew, one of her sunning herself on the beach in a tiny bikini, and finally, one of her giving me a piggy back ride.

Eventually, I got enough courage to enter the room where my buddy lay, motionless. She was just lying there, in almost the same position as the last time I saw her. I sat in the seat next to her bed, and grabbed her cool, emaciated hand. I sat and stroked it while I talked to her. Of course she gave me no response, but then again, I didn't expect one. I still don't even know if she heard the words that I said. For a while, she opened her eyes: her pain, suffering, and her desire to escape it all, the way they sparkled blue made me forget, just for a brief moment, that my buddy was dying. I could not help but wonder if she could see me. The one in the middle, I thought to myself. Then she shut them. "I love you," I whispered. I got up, leaned over, and kissed her cheek. My tears rolling down my face, then hers.

When I turned and walked away, I knew that would be the last time that I would see my friend with any remains of life left in her. The next morning, I was called out of class by the principal. Words were not necessary. I knew what had happened. The battle that Debs had been fighting for eight months had finally come to an end. Instantly, I began crying. I made my way to his office where my mom approached me with her own tears. "I'm sorry," was all that she said. I sat and cried until my tears ran dry.

At the wake, I caught one last glimpse of my buddy. She looked beautiful. A blond wig was placed upon her bald head, her nails were perfectly painted, and she had on her favorite Manasquan basketball sweatshirt. In the gleaming gold coffin she lay still. Her promising blue eyes that were once able to reveal her world were resting shut, now hollow and lifeless. For the last time, I held her hand, which was cold and still. Swarms of people with tears and swollen eyes came to say their goodbyes. Cancer had the power to take Debs away from me physically, but in my heart, my mind, and my actions she will always be present.

After watching my best friend wither away from such a terrible disease at only seventeen, I began to think a great deal about my life, and life in general. I now realized that living is a privilege. We always think that because we are so young, we will live to be old. Well, then again why would we have reason to believe that our life would be cut short? We always think of the future, yet never imagine that there is a possibility that we will not have the opportunity to live it.

In our fast-paced society, where there is an enormous amount of pressure upon us to succeed, it is very easy to lose touch with the present. Almost everything that we do is for some type of future success. Often, we find ourselves stressing out over grades, money, and relationships, and fail to enjoy many parts of life. We watch life pass us by. The present becomes a blur. We definitely must plan for the future, but at the same time we must continue to celebrate each day.

We should make time to enjoy the simple pleasures of life that we tend to take for granted. Make a point of making yourself happy. Make a point of opening your eyes to see just how beautiful the gift of life is. Ask yourself, if your life were to end today, would you be content with how you have spent your time? If not, make a point of changing your life. Fill your days with smiles and laughter. With each breath you breathe, you should become drunk on your existence. Bring yourself to life! Love living, while you still have the opportunity to.

In a way, life in the present era is very similar to the basketball games that Debs and I once played together. We played them from beginning to end, each moment attempting to find the strategy that would put us on top. We were always looking for that one move that would make us victorious. Essentially, that is what the entire game is about, winning in the end. It doesn't matter what the score is at half-time or even in the last seconds of the game. But unlike a basketball game, in the sport of life, we are not guaranteed a full game. In life we must concentrate on the present, for at any time the whistle may blow.

The Shore

Eric Dechtiaruk
Spring 1998 – Volume XIX

I am at the Shore. As I walk across the flat back yard my shoes are moistened with the morning dew, where the golden sun is refracting into a thousand tiny rainbows. The lawn seems to be more clover than grass. On both sides of the back yard are my grandfather's gardens. The rows of tomato plants held in form by cylindrical wire cages, the trellis of cucumber, rows of string beans, and skirts of sunflowers all give the air the sweet scent of new life. They seem to give off their own emerald radiance that floats solidly through the air and gives me a warm, cozy feeling inside.

The previous times I have come down to the Shore are awakened in my mind. But it is more a sense of having been part of this place than anything else. I remember the rides on our Bayliner Classic. I remember the excursions in our fiberglass boat. The pull of the current, power of the wind, and fear of the storm that chased me across the Bay are all engraved in my being. They are as much a part of me as I am a part of the human race.

"Aunt, do you want to go for a ride with me?" I ask as she sits in the lawn chair on top of the hill.

She puts down her cup of tea and *Newsweek* magazine. "Sure," she replies.

I endanger my own life in carrying the heavy, "one-armed man," the white Johnson outboard, down the steep hill. I run out back to get the fuel canister and inside to get the oars and the life preservers.

As I step onto the sun-bleached pier and gaze across Old Road Bay at Bethlehem Steel, fire inside of me flares up just a bit. But I avoid looking into it, avoid trying to think about what it is, and attach the motor to the hand-powered hoist used to lower it onto the yellow, fiberglass boat which rests sturdily atop the calm water. Each year the water is a little cleaner, thanks to pollution-control laws implemented at Bethlehem Steel. It is not your ordinary saltwater. It seems to be a living thing as it swells and sinks ever so subtly. The afternoon sun penetrates about two feet down, giving it the same internal radiance as my grandfather's garden, the front porch and the lawn.

But I slow down my hurried pace when a weight seems to pull down on my heart. It is a kind of burning, like a fire deep down inside, that blazes up when I realize I've been taking the splendor of this place for granted. But it is somehow more than just this. It is as if just as I reach a kind of ecstasy of joy, I question myself as to whether I really should be happy or not. It feels as if something is inside me and has its claws compressed around my heart. I turn to glance up at the blazing sun, then I turn around and scan my surroundings as slight fear, or insecurity, trickles into me. But as I notice the way the sun filters through the green foliage and throws golden spots on the lawn; the way the light illuminates the front porch as a cool breeze drifts through the screens surrounding the porch; the look of love on my aunt's face; all help to quench the fire inside me. It takes a lot of effort, but I keep it below the surface.

After working a few minutes to get the motor on the boat and make sure we are ready, I unharness the boat and jump in with my aunt. Now the fun begins. I connect the black rubber handle of the starter cord. The two-cylinder outboard springs to life with a warm, blue-white cloud of smoke. It smells heavenly, and brings to mind the exact same feeling of peace and purpose that I've had every other time I've started this outboard.

It takes fairly quick reflexes to respond to the sputtering in time. I release the starter cord from my left hand and quickly move it down the front of the motor and close the choke, reducing the amount of oxygen available for combustion. With my right hand, I rapidly turn the throttle counterclockwise before the engine starves from a lack of air. The outboard produces a furious roar accompanied by an even larger cloud of blue-white smoke. Just a little slower, I turn back the throttle and push the shift lever into forward. This all takes about fifteen to twenty seconds.

We're off. Gray rolls seamlessly into a brighter saltwater blue, and covers the surface of the earth for miles. As I look to the south, out across the water, I can make out the outline of the Bay Bridge. Old Road Bay opens into the Patapsco right at the river's mouth. The Patapsco pours into the Chesapeake Bay. At the end of the Patapsco is the Inner Harbor of Baltimore City. Across the river, the houses are merely white spots along the shoreline. The shape of Old Road Bay is like a gigantic puzzle piece, with three dead end creeks offering sanctuary for a hundred or so seafaring crafts. Occasionally, usually on weekends, a dozen of these will dare to wander out of their ports and slip beyond the Bay into the adjoining Chesapeake or up into the Patapsco towards Baltimore City. With its gentle touch, the water brushes against the aging wood pilings and bulkheads which hold the land against erosion. A comforting arrangement of quaint households rests gently along the zigzag shore. Each has its own unique shape and age. I often wonder how many other great-grandfathers started with little wooden shacks. These houses are offered shade by thousands of oak and maple trees which seem to get lighter and lighter the farther away they are. And across from the remnants of a tiny, tattered, overgrown beach looms Bethlehem Steel on Sparrows Point.

Towering smoke stacks, vast mountains of tan sand and pitch-black coal by the docks on the mouth of the Patapsco, warehouses, and a maze of roadways all encompass one of the largest steel factories on the east coast. A long, deep roar, like that of a dragon waking from sleep, echoes across the Bay as the monstrous blast furnace spews out steels by some ancient, mystical process. I often pause for a moment and wonder which has been here longer, the land or Bethlehem Steel. I cannot ignore the awesome grandeur of this place. This place where steam bellows up and meets the banquet of fluffy white clouds as they gracefully glide across the deep blue sky that makes you wish the world would turn upside-down so you can fall into it. And the sun! The splendor of the sun gives a golden clarity to everything – from the lighthouse at Fort Howard on the edge of the Bay to Wagner Station across the Patapsco. Not your ordinary golden sun, but a crisp ball of fire that stretches its arms in between the clouds and touches the earth with its fingertips. I have returned to the cries of the osprey and the mysterious bellow of the heron.

I have, to date, found no way to describe the utter joy and peace that settles in me here. This is where the world dons its halo and combines distance and perspective, light and shadow, steel and earth, to show all that life is about. "The Shore" no longer seems to be simply the "perfect place." It seems to be alive, and how I long to be alive with it. I often feel like Cortez or Columbus must have when they first discovered the New World. I am always overwhelmed with a sense that I belong here.

I feel like the Shore is holding something in store for me, and it fills me with both excitement and fear. Fear rising from the occasional thought that "it's just me;" that I am getting a little carried away. My family and friends always told me I had an overactive imagination. But if I am not crazy, then why is my joy mingled with fear? Why is this fire inside me? After all, no one else seems to see this place the way I do. My friends back home thought it was "nice," or "peaceful," or "quiet," but they never seemed to enjoy it very much (they always expected a lot of bikini-clad women). When I would tell them that there is no phone, no movie theater, no cable TV, the excitement would leak from their eyes and they would usually decline my invitation.

But as I gaze at Bethlehem Steel, I once again feel a tension increase inside me. The burning returns as I wonder whether I am really in awe of what I am seeing; if I am enjoying it, or if I even should be. As we near the plant, everything – the wind, the waves, the perspective – changes. I do not know whether to enjoy it more the way it appeared a minute ago, or whether to abandon that joy for the new one that lies ahead of me.

My ailment has been given a name: obsessive-compulsive disorder. Instead of wanting to wash my hands over and over again, though, I need to pray over and over again. It is very hard to describe, and even harder to understand. What makes it so peculiar is that I am convinced that mine is actually a struggle on a spiritual level, as if, for some reason, I can only look at what I can enjoy, or if something is keeping me from enjoying it. But even if this is true, it is the nature of OCD to have me doubting myself.

"Eric," comes my aunt's soft voice over the roar of the outboard. Part of me wishes she would just shut up and leave me alone to figure this out. But at the same time,

I desperately need her support. "Eric, God knows you thank Him for this place."

I grit my teeth and holler back over the roar of the motor, "Then why do I feel this way?"

"God is NOT a feeling! You have to fight this!"

"I AM!"

I muster as much courage as I can as the Shore is torn of its appeal. I concentrate on the fire inside me and say to it, "There is nothing you can do to me that has not already been done." Just as the Shore seems to be becoming as bland as a block in the inner city, colorless, filthy, polluted, I realized that this could not, would not have happened anywhere else, and I am reminded of the fabled phoenix.

Rapidly, the fire seems to rush out of me and releases its great store of anxiety and tension. I look out over Old Road Bay at Bethlehem Steel and I know that I am not crazy. I am no longer afraid that all of a sudden, for no apparent reason, the Shore will lose its special meaning to me. The Shore regains its "heavenly radiance," but it is not quite as mystical. It is just as breathtaking as a few moments ago, but its ability to inspire awe seems to be sure. I feel reassured that no matter what happens, the Shore will be able to give me at least some peace and relaxation. I am becoming a firm believer in the idea that "nothing is a coincidence." It is not a coincidence that the seed should land in the right spot and begin its growth. Or is it?

Lavender & Old Ladies

Alexandra J. Feigel
Spring 2000 – Volume XXI

I lived with my great grandmother for the first eight years of my life, but I still wonder weather she ever figured out my name. That's just the way she was. She had twenty-three great grandchildren to keep track of, and even at the ripe old age of 85 (which I will always consider to have been her prime), she could rattle off the name of every single one before she got to mine. It never bothered me, except when I was in a hurry; her backwards record player sounding chain of half-names seemed to last an hour. I can still hear her squealing from the kitchen, "Rich-Kel-Kev-Es-Lis-Ed-Wal-Jen, get in here and clean your plate," as I was running off to catch a chicken or build a tree house. It may have been that I was just a kid, and remembering my name wasn't that big a deal to me, but now, looking back, I realize that Great Grandma and I had a connection deeper than I have ever had with any other human being. Great Grandma was more than a mom, dad, brother, mentor, or even a great grandma. Above all, she was my friend.

I spent weeks, sometimes months at a time, at Great Grandma's. Mom and Dad would wake me up at our house very early, so they could drop me off and be at work on time. It wasn't a big deal, and we didn't make it a big deal because then it would seem like they were leaving me. By doing the drop-off quickly and painlessly, my parents tried to downplay the situation. I was always eager to go to Great Grandma's, although I often pleaded with my parents to let me take Kevin, my older brother, with me. Kevin was in all-day school, and although he sometimes came for the weekends, he came on his own will, for fun, and that was a completely different concept. I had fun at Great Grandma's, but originally, it wasn't my decision to go there.

It wasn't that my parents abandoned me or didn't want me, they just wanted to make sure that I had a "normal" kid's life, with plenty of love and attention. After my mother's maternity leave was up, she had to go right back to work or risk not advancing in her career. The same was true for my father. They didn't really try to explain it to me; after all, I was only three months old when I went to Great Grandma's for the first time. After that, it was old hat. Sometimes, Mom and Dad were "off to work" with a kiss, wink, and a smile. Other times they were "very, very busy. Daddy's got a new client, darling." They meant well, I know that now – they weren't making excuses for their good, but rather for mine. They were torn between building a good home or just being with me. Their decision to send me to Great Grandma's was the best move they could have ever made.

Great Grandma was too old to work, so instead she managed her farm a half-hour outside Pittsburgh, where my parents lived. Great Grandma and I stayed in the main house. She had her own room downstairs next to the kitchen, and I had mine, up the stairs and to the left. Mine was a beautiful, sprawling room, decidedly southern in character. Yellow floral drapes framed two huge windows, and homemade, overstuffed pillows stretched the length of the window seats. An ebony armoire occupied one corner, a vanity sat against the wall opposite the door and a huge canopy bed was on another wall. It too was covered with Great Grandma's hand-stitched yellow sheets and pillow shams. Her trademarked patchwork quilt covered the foot of the bed, and baby dolls and stuffed animals (also completely homemade) sat on my pillows. My room seemed to catch the sunlight at any time of the day, whether to accompany the rooster every morning or to embrace me as I said my evening prayers.

Great Grandma was the one who decided my room would be southern – she came from the Deep South, a small town in Georgia that has since been swallowed up by industry and expansion. She was born in 1902 into a poor, farming family. They lived in a small, one-room house among fields and fields of her father's tobacco. When she was five, her father died, and Great Grandma watched his proud, busy tobacco wither as her mother planned her second marriage. Years later, when she was eight, her mother died giving birth to her twin brother and sister. She became the caretaker of the new babies. When the twins were old enough to require more solid food, Great Grandma would chew up meat and then feed it to them. She would only chew on bones to satisfy her hunger. On their second birthday, the twins died in their sleep. The day after, her stepfather dropped Great Grandma off at her grandparents' and left town. When they didn't want her anymore, she went to her aunt and uncle's home in northern Georgia. When Great Grandma turned eighteen, she decided that she had had enough shuffling around.

Luckily, it was at that point that she met my great grandfather, Ferdinand Vanistendael, a Belgian who spoke perfect English. He was on his way to Pittsburgh, the city of steel mills. He asked her if he could take her away from Georgia and marry her. She, of course, said yes, and on April 18th, 1920, Essie Mae Mathews became Essie Mae Vanistendael in a small Catholic Church in

Pittsburgh near her new home. My great grandfather set her free, took her away, and loved her when she felt only anger at being constantly abandoned. Although I never met him, I will forever admire him for this, as he taught Great Grandma to do the same for me.

I can't remember the first day I went to Great Grandma's to stay for an extended period, although I do remember a time I returned after being with Mom, Dad, and my brother Kevin for Christmas. I was about six years old, red and green ribbons flowed through my blond hair, and my bright eyes were anxiously waiting to get back to my farm. What would the cats and the horses do without me for one more day? My father walked me from the tan Thunderbird; we trudged through the snow, me in my multi-colored moon boots and mended, hand-me-down coat, he in his gray wool overcoat. Dad tripped over the ledge leading to the door, the ledge I was so accustomed to running over, and I wondered what was wrong with him. As I pulled open the screen door, the smell of the wood fire wafted through my numb nostrils. Dad brushed off my boots and helped me up onto the doorstep. The familiar and unmistakable smell of home flew from the stove; Great Grandma was making me sweet potato pie. Dad squatted down outside the door, and I stood facing him, a few steps away inside the kitchen. He smiled and said, "Whatcha thinking, Jen-girl?" I sighed, and replied, "It's good to be home." Even through his fogged up glasses I could see the desperate flash of shocked sadness pass through his eyes. Great Grandma turned away, toward the sink, and began to wash dishes. Dad didn't say anything for a moment, and I just stood there. Finally, he kissed me, said "I love you," and left. He wasn't angry, he had just realized that Great Grandma's was my home.

My relationship with Great Grandma centered on the fact that she let me be independent, to grow because of my own decisions and their outcomes, not the typical, "Don't do that" way of learning. I made my own schedule, and knew what my responsibilities were. As long as I fulfilled my end of the unspoken bargain, she and I would be fine. Also, Great Grandma never made me feel like I was a visitor. Everything she had was mine; it was our home. If there was any unspoken exchange, it was simply my unconditional love for her.

A typical day began at the crack of dawn; we got up with the roosters. Great Grandma would make flapjacks with molasses, or steaming grits with orange or peach marmalade. She steamed milk on the stove every morning and made me fresh hot cocoa. Then we were on our way. First, we fed the chickens, they bothered you the most, and Great Grandma hated to be pecked on the legs. Then we poured milk over old bread for the cats, gave Skippy, my horse, his morning oats and hay, and then fed the cows and ducks. I raced back to the house to get my backpack, filled to the brim with the essentials for any child's day of adventure: a hammer, bent and discarded nails, crayons, a few bottles of warm Coke, lots of damp, black mud, worms, and my great grandfather's pocket watch which had an engraving to Great Grandma on it. That went in the clean front pocket for safekeeping. Then I was off. I would saddle up my Skippy and set off for that day's task, whether to build a clubhouse or rig a tree swing.

Great Grandma and I ate lunch together every day; often she packed a basket and brought it up to the hillside that I would play on. We would lie on the blanket, and she would rattle off all the tall tales and true-life stories she knew. My favorite was the one about the three-legged dog named Champ that she had as a child. A three-legged dog was very interesting to me, for some reason. When I got upset and cried about my failed attempt at a duck trap she would laugh at me and make up a silly rhyme. When

I made her angry, instead of yelling she would silence my arguing by crying, "Snot, snot, eat it red hot!" We would both collapse in laughter, she, an 85-year-old retired nurse, and I, a seven-year-old tomboy raised on a farm.

I didn't have to come in at night until I wanted to; Great Grandma thought I should make my own decisions. All she said was to watch for coyotes and raccoons, and not to let the devil catch my toes, digging in the ground after dark. That warning alone had me inside no later than an hour after sundown, or ten o'clock. Besides, Great Grandma and I had stuff to do. First I had my bath, then I would run, steam rising from my little body to her room, where she dressed me in my great grandpa's old, dingy undershirts which I used as nightgowns. If I was lucky, I got to put on her silky powder, a luxury after a hard day's work. It smelled of lavender and old ladies, a smell that grabs me even today, if I'm lucky enough to come across it.

Stories and songs, and hot milk with vanilla and cinnamon marked nighttime with Great Grandma. She would lie with me and rub my back until I fell asleep. She covered me with the quilt she had made, and kissed my forehead. Sometimes, I would wake up as she left the room. I could hear her groan as she went down the steps; they were so hard on her arthritis. That didn't matter to her, though. Every night, no matter what, she did her routine.

I moved out when I was eight. My parents decided that it was time to stay at home; I was to go to a new school. I left, kicking and screaming, and, as usual, Great Grandma stayed calm, assuring me I'd be back the next summer to stay. She was right, I would come back the next summer and all the summers after that, and things always went back to normal. We fell back into our old routine and I was happy again. Winters away from Great

Grandma were rough. In the beginning, I had a bit of a southern drawl, and I used all of Great Grandma's odd phrases. The kids at school always made fun of me, and embarrassed, my parents constantly corrected my grammar. It didn't matter to me, though, because Great Grandma had taught me tolerance, patience, and the beauty of taking things with a grain of salt.

Great Grandma died when I was thirteen; she was ninety years old. She had suffered through three strokes, which left her almost entirely blind, and paralyzed her left leg. Because of this she had to go live with my grandmother, and I knew this was hard for Great Grandma, as she never wanted to be thrown into anyone's lap ever again. However, she stayed strong. She didn't show her pain and kept the pride I so admired. Inside, I was miserable. Great Grandma and I could never again have our routine; she would never again watch the sunset with me on a red and white checkered tablecloth while we talked about fireflies and crazy black roosters. She would never again walk me up the stairs to bed. Just when I got desperate, and was clawing at some remainder of our past, I realized Great Grandma still couldn't get my name, ever, even on the fifth or sixth try. In an odd and confusing way, it comforted me.

After Great Grandma's death, I felt as if a chair had been pulled out from under me. Although she couldn't walk, and rarely spoke near the end of her life, she still inspired me and kept me strong. When she died, I felt truly abandoned for the first time. Every day after her death, for months, I wrote letters to her in a notebook. I reminded her of all the things we used to do, and how much fun we had. I told her how sad I was that she died. I pasted pictures of her and me together, feeding the horses or shoveling manure. I asked her to give me some sign that she heard me because I couldn't understand where she had gone. At times, I got angry with her for leaving me. I assumed that since she had taken me when my parents didn't want me, that meant she would never leave me. I thought that when she did leave, she would at least let me down easy. She was the first person I ever knew that died, and when she did, there was no one there to explain it to me. For my family to justify my sadness would be to admit that I was really close to her. And admitting that I was really that close to her was admitting that they had abandoned me and allowed our closeness to start.

As children, we are all relatively sheltered, which allows us to believe that the life we are living is completely normal, and is the same as every other kid's we see on the streets. I did see kids with their parents more often than I saw them with great grandparents, but I justified it somehow. Because of this, abandonment is something you feel only if you can comprehend it and are conscious of it, but is often only apparent in the eye of the onlooker. I'm sure many of my relatives and family friends who knew my situation pitied me, but I never felt sad. I don't understand where their pity came from, and in a way, I resent it. By pitying me, it was as if they were saying I wasn't normal, and that I was missing out, but I wasn't. Great Grandma was my life. The farm was our life. Our adventures were what kept us alive. We were each other's happiness.

At Great Grandma's funeral, the song she had chosen as her recessional was "The Wind Beneath My Wings." Although the song was written about faith, it was also the song of our relationship. In the song, the "you" is the person who helps the other person to fly. She is the wind, unable to be seen, but yet so strong. Birds depend on the wind to propel them to flight, just as we depended on each other. By ourselves, we were completely independent, because of the lives in which we had both been abandoned. But when we came together, ironically, we became weak, and depended too much on one another.

I have never been as close to another human being as I was to Great Grandma. She taught me what true devotion and companionship really is. She taught me independence and self-sufficiency, but didn't allow those difficult lessons from a person who knew the ins and outs of my heart but never really knew my name.

Once, at a father-daughter lunch at Cozumel, my favorite Mexican restaurant, my dad apologized for choices that he made that had hurt me while I was growing up, and then asked if I thought he was a bad parent. It was a difficult question to answer, as I knew exactly what he was talking about. I knew that, as a parent, it was his nature to agonize over every decision he made while I was growing up. I also knew that all his fears were unfounded, and I reassured him of this. However, as I reflect on this moment in relation to the rest of my life, I wonder if this was the correct conclusion. I don't know if all his decisions benefited me; all I know is that today, I am Jen, and that is all that matters.

I don't know if a child's place is with her mother and father. Nor do I know if her place is with her Great Grandmother. For all I know, a child belongs with a pack of wolves or a family of lions. I'm not an expert on child psychology, and I don't think anybody really is. We only know that a certain moment or decision in life is right if we are living it, if we are feeling it at that given moment. Looking back and analyzing decisions made more than a decade ago serves no beneficial purpose; instead it leads to regret and sometimes remorse. I don't ever want my parents to think that they've done me any wrong by having sent me to live with my Great Grandma, because they didn't. They are the only ones who question my well being today, as they are the ones who made the decision those

18 years ago.

I wish there were a few choice words to sum this up, to give closure to the abandonment issue, but I can't. I don't know whether I was abandoned. Because I don't *feel* as if I was abandoned, I find it hard to define this word for myself, let alone other people. The bottom line is that I was lucky enough as a child to have been shaped by many dynamic people and experiences. Great Grandma would surely go at the top of that list, but my father, my brother, fireflies, my retarded friend Boo (not Radley), my friends today, and my five-month-old niece Kristen would follow. I am still a child, in a way, and I am still developing. We are constantly being influenced, by people and experiences, and we often try to comprehend this concept. Our development as people is not meant to be monitored and analyzed, it is meant to be left alone. Our thriving as humans should be allowed to blossom and turn into something beautiful that we are not necessarily meant to understand. Life was not intended to be planned and made perfect. All we are meant to do is live.

Valentine's Day Apostle

Jenny Zasowski
Spring 2000 – Volume XXI

Today is not only a Saturday, it is Valentine's Day and driving my sister's red Chrysler Concorde, I am headed to Prospect Avenue to pick up my friend Chrissy. My first stop is marked by the precision between the white lines of the Quick Check parking lot. A few minutes later, I emerge from this place of "convenience" with French Vanilla coffee – a drink that supposedly "stunts my growth," yet helps ease the transition to the adult world. I have secret, important matters to take care of, matters that make me feel mature in the early daylight. They are issues that ten minutes ago forced me to sneak out of my house and deceive my parents. Above all, I just want to do what is best for Chrissy.

She gives me a warm smile as she slowly walks towards the car parked outside her house. After strapping on the seatbelt, she faces me and gives me a heartfelt "Thanks." I casually reply, "No problem." We begin our journey with the soothing voice of Adam Duritz and our favorite song "Round Here" in the background.

Chrissy directs me from a square yellow note paper that she clutches tightly the entire time. The New Jersey Turnpike, Route 287…forty minutes later, and before I can breathe in all I have ever been taught in life, we are here. Sitting in the parked car in what appears to be an affluent neighborhood, I find it difficult to focus on the name of the establishment on the sign. I can't stop look-ing at this small group of dedicated protesters with hand-made posters raised proudly in the air. They are slowly parading in a circle outside the building. I instantly feel paralyzed, saddened, sick, and worse, I feel stuck.

"C'mon," she says, as she can probably see me begin-ning to fade away. The street light is red as we step out of the car. I put a quarter in the meter, and we cross the street in front of a shiny, black Volvo, towards the small but powerful clan of believers. One of them comes to meet us. Desperately trying to work her magic, she wants to "talk things over." Her name is Barbara and she *knows* that "there is another way." Politely, we give Barbara some of our time. She quotes the Bible and wants us to trust in God. With a Styrofoam cup of coffee in one hand, she reaches around with the other to pull out a pamphlet from the back pocket of her jeans. Pointing to the list under the subtitle "Alternatives," she asks if we would like a cup of coffee of our own, her "treat," so that we can sit down to discuss our options in more detail. I uneasily look to Chrissy, who is staring at "Today's Special" posted on the dry-erase board outside the gourmet shop. Barely looking back at Barbara, I decline.

"Which one of you is it?" Barbara abruptly asks as we begin to walk away. The three of us now at a halt, she focuses on Chrissy, who shakes her head from left to right in denial. From this point on, Barbara directs all of her talk at me. She comes closer and preaches to me from her own experiences. She, too, once brought a friend to an abortion clinic and feels it heavily on her conscience even now. Standing there, listening to her talk, I am unable to shake this one thought from my head and, as a result, I feel silently condescending: *thank God I am still a virgin… thank God I am not the one who is pregnant…* My smug smile fades as she implores, "Please don't do this."

Her request makes me uncomfortable. I am irritable because deep down I can *feel* that Barbara is right – and here I am supporting what my parents and a lot of other people think is wrong. This woman who, minutes ago, was a stranger, has got me holding conversations in my head. *That's right, Jenny. Stay stone-faced. Don't for a second think that you helping out a friend in need is wrong – and for that reason alone you are doing the right thing.*

Barbara's brown eyes are sincere, but I sympathize with Chrissy, who demonstrates her certainty by straying away from Barbara. Following her lead only takes me even closer to the gang of other protesters. "Look at what you are doing. Please reconsider!" yells the middle-aged woman with blond hair and black roots carrying a picture of a fetus. "We can help you!" shouts a younger woman. "Don't do this!" begs a third. Two steps later and we are "safe" at the door.

Chrissy goes right to the front desk of the L-shaped room to fill out the papers and pay for the procedure, while I turn the corner to find a seat in the crowded waiting room of the second floor. *Men in Black* is playing on the television and I desperately try to lose myself in the scene. My efforts are unsuccessful as Will Smith is searching for clues to a murder at a morgue; the concept only makes me worry more about where I am right now. Barbara's words start echoing and the time is running short. *I take pride in how great a kid I am, so what am I doing here? I was wrong: I don't belong here.*

I look around at all the unfamiliar faces, and, with tearing eyes, start to panic when I cannot find Chrissy among the other patients. *Did she go in already? Please God, no. Let me speak my piece.* I stand up and my legs make contact with all those sitting down as I make my way towards the desk. One Hispanic couple, both in their mid-twenties, halts their conversation and look up at me as I hurriedly pass by. I imagine their wonderment surrounding the circumstances that brought me to this place.

Turning the corner, I find Chrissy blank-faced, leaning against the wall.

"I need to talk to you," I say, damned near hysterical. "I don't want you to do this. I thought I could handle taking you here, but I was wrong. Chrissy, I don't want to be here. Please reconsider."

She speaks without emotion as though she is unmoved by my gravity. "Jenny, I'm sorry that you feel this way, but I'm gonna go through with it. If I don't do it now, the cost increases. I have no other choice. You can leave if you want, and I'll find another way home."

Now I am scared out of my mind. Here I am breaking down, while Chrissy remains strong as she typically does in the face of adversity.

She and I have been playing basketball together for five years. This year, our senior season found me as captain and her as my assistant until midway through when she decided to quit. Between living in her sister's shadow on the court and the frequent embarrassment caused by her father's public rage each time the coach screamed at her for making a mistake, Chrissy said she couldn't handle playing anymore. After a close win at Middletown North High School, while most of the parents stood congregated on the gym floor excitedly talking about the game, Chrissy's father was causing something to talk about on his own. As our victorious coach accepted the congratulations while making his way towards the locker room, Chrissy's dad began kicking the bleachers and loudly calling him an "asshole," swearing that his daughter "shouldn't have been benched the second half!" Despite Chrissy's stoic façade during coach's post-game wrap up, she turned in her uniform the next day. "I have to do what's best for me," she explained to me in home-room that morning…

*Well what about what's best for **me** right now?* I started thinking about the constant pressure that my parents put on me to always "do the right thing." I'm not so sure that I'm doing it right now. I need someone to help me get through this, but looking around at the strangers in the waiting room leaves me no better off. No way am I going to abandon Chrissy, but I need to do something for myself.

Alone, I go down the stairs and out into the cold, crisp air. The picketers are in the spot where we left them, but this time appear less monstrous and more human. It is as if they were taking a break – no shouting of convictions, just a few of them engaged in some intimate conversation. I take a deep breath as I quickly try to slip by.

The hawk-like Barbara won't let me go unnoticed, though. She immediately rushes over, as I increase my speed. The pace proves a little too much for her, and from a step or so behind, she joyfully wants to know if I reconsidered. "Where are you going?" she hounds me.

Unsure of what I will actually do, I escape to the red car. To make it look as if I have a plan, I grab a handful of change out of the ashtray. After flipping the visor down, I stare at myself in the mirror, marveling at the reflection for a second. *I thought I knew who you were…* I angrily slap it back up, then get out of the car.

Barbara loyally joins me when I get back to her ter-ritory on the other side of the street. She starts talking again, and now feeling more lost than ever before in my life, I listen. "Thank God…" she is still chirping about the decision she thinks I have made. "Don't worry, we will find a way to help you," she rejoices. Annoyed at myself for having given her false hope, I rudely shut her up by saying, "It's not me! I'm not the one getting it done!" Poor

Barbara, she thought herself victorious for a while; the saint thought she had saved another soul.

I continue to talk, tears now streaming down my face. "I don't want her to do it, but she won't listen to me. I'm so scared. I don't know what to do and I don't know who to call."

Right then and there, Barbara starts praying out loud on the cobblestone sidewalk. I have my hands wrapped around the receiver of the pay phone and bow my head, searching for anyone's grace. *"Dear God, please give Jenny here the strength and answer to the question of who she should call…"*

I'm sobbing, thinking of the utter disappointment my Catholic parents will have in me. I'm so afraid of them, of how their view of their baby girl will change. I feel the fear, but call anyway.

"Mom?" I say in a trembling voice.

"Where are you?" I can tell she has been heavily concerned.

"I'm so sorry, Mom. I'm so sorry…" I'm crying with Barbara right beside me.

"Jenny, where are you?" I know she is afraid of my response.

"Please don't be mad at me, and don't judge or think less of Chrissy. Mom, I took Chrissy to get an abortion…" I put my head down and close my eyes, preparing for her response.

"Oh, Jenny…" She wants to know exactly where I am so she can come and pick me up.

"No, Mom. I'm not going to tell you. I don't want you to come." I'm still crying, but feel better because she now knows the truth behind my earlier disappearance. "I'll be okay, I just don't want you to be mad. I'm sorry. I'm sorry, Mom."

"Jenny, I'm not mad at you right now, but I do want

to be there for you." I tell her again that despite the way I sound now, "I'll be okay." I don't want her to come, because I want some time for myself to reflect on this experience.

I hang up the phone and while wiping away some tears, look towards heaven. After taking a deep breath, my gaze shifts back towards the angel Barbara. Peacefully, she smiles and reaches out to hug me.

She asks me again if I would like a cup of coffee, and I take her up on the offer this time. She goes first into one of those gourmet shops and holds the door open for me. The stylish man in the tight, ribbed black turtleneck, black rimmed glasses, and apron at the cash register knows her by name. "The usual, Barb?" he asks. "And what about for her?"

I go for plain coffee this time and while we sit there, she tells me a little about herself. Barbara was once very promiscuous, but now she believes she has "seen the light." She is dedicated to helping others find a way as well, and is delighted when she hears I am still a virgin.

Twenty-five minutes later, there are two empty cups on the table. I thank Barbara for the time she has spent helping me, and she leaves me with her copy of the Bible. She inscribes a personal message on the inside of the paperback cover, a sentiment her black ink makes most permanent in my mind, "Waiting is worth it..."

I ascend those stairs again and pass the Hispanic couple who watch me as they did during my panic before. Sitting alone in the still-crowded waiting room, I notice that not much has changed except for the fact that Chrissy isn't around. She's somewhere behind the double doors; through anesthesia she has temporarily transcended the world.

Noticing the heart stickies on the window for the first time, I am reminded of the irony of the day – St.

Valentine's Day. Sitting there, my mind wanders off to the purpose of its celebration, the different chambers of love: romantic, physical, brotherly, spiritual, and unconditional. I conclude that when we have self and spiritual love, it is easier to stay away from the physical. I then wonder what kind of love all the people in the room around me have in their life, and I say a prayer for all the positive love I am fortunate enough to have in mine.

About an hour later, the double doors open and a nurse is showing Chrissy the way out. She stops to look around the room, probably a little unsure of whether or not I'd be there. Her doubts are erased when we make eye contact as I stand up and start moving towards her. She tries to give me that smile she did when coming out of her house earlier in the morning, but her façade can't hide the pain this time. It even hurts to look at her for she seems very weak. Slightly hunched over, she strugglingly walks towards me.

We meet and I instantly give her a hug. I don't completely let go, but instead keep my arm around her as a source of support. Looking at the nurse I say, "Thanks...I have it from here."

On Satires, Racism, and the World in General

James Beaver
Spring 2001 – Volume XXII

I can say this – it started out as a kind of joke. I thought it was funny, strange, and just bizarre at some points. When I say this "joke," I am referring to what later developed into my essay on racism. Basically, the joke started out as a radical idea of "killing off" all of the races in America in order to end racism. I thought about it at first and said, "No way." No way could I write something so volatile, so daring, on a topic as explosive as racism. I personally feel that the racism issue in America is a powder keg. Most people want to "solve" it or take different approaches at understanding it, but we have to be careful not to offend anybody or come too close. Nobody likes to light matches next to dynamite.

Where can we find the answer then? How could I write something different? Something new? God knows it is easy for me, as a white male from South Jersey, to talk about how we should all treat each other fairly. I think of who I really am now, since I have written the essay. The answer is quite clear to me: I am comfortably white – I have experienced nothing directly that has led me to understand racism better. By comfortably white I mean that I have lived in a sheltered home – the "typical" white American home. By comfortable I mean that I never have had to sit in the back of a bus, never have had difficulty hailing a cab, and never been mocked for slanted eyes (because I have "normal eyes"). I seem to always be in the majority, never really feeling outwardly different.

Racism, for me, is an issue – not a slap in the face; that is, it has never hit me. As part of the white majority in the United States, I have always observed how racism simply flies above me and always lands on "someone else." In fact, racism never fails to direct itself toward that "someone else," and not me. Not a white child from New Jersey. I feel typically white. Maybe I am wrong, but this is the feeling I had when I searched for something to write on racism. How could I write about this issue? I might have seen it, but I have never felt it or touched it (I have not delivered racist remarks nor been hit with them). I searched for ideas, but in the back of my mind I only discovered emptiness. I felt as if anything I could write would not dive into the problem – it would just float on the surface for me (and the reader for that matter).

Well, I could offer my suggestion on how I think we should "solve" the problem. Oh, here's a good one – let all the ethnic groups get together for a Sunday night dinner, talk, and become friends. Great. Surely, if I can think it and do it, we all should be able to come together. I think that is obviously not so simple. Can you see what I mean? Do you know where I am coming from? If I suggested something like this, I would end up choking on the plastic of my own words and phrases. It would be so fake; even worse, it would be so simplistic.

So there it is – my justification for putting the "crazy joke" onto paper. Something different, I thought. The joke itself made me chuckle in an unsettling manner – was it really humorous? I decided that I would slowly show how to destroy the physical differences between people in order to attain racial harmony. That was not the funny part, though. The real humor, I thought, existed in the idea that no one would be left at the end of the plan. The destruction of all races would lead to an empty world, but racial harmony would be achieved. Now that I think about it, it may not be so funny. If that is the only way to achieve racial harmony on earth then I am certainly not laughing. But I was laughing before I wrote this essay, and instead of questioning the logic behind it, I spent many restless nights trying to determine how I could do it.

One of these nights, I remembered Jonathan Swift's *A Modest Proposal*, the satire in which he proposes that the English make use of Irish babies as wholesome entrees. That was it. That was enough for me. A satire. A fresh perspective. Something different. Something that would knock the reader off his or her feet.

With this idea of writing a satire in a similar manner as Swift's work, I sat down at my computer around eight o'clock on a Thursday night. I had written nothing on paper yet, but then I guess I had never intended to do so. The plastic letters on the keyboard were perfect pieces to convey my thoughts. In fact, I could not write the essay on paper first…writing with ink on paper to me is like a pouring out of my soul, but this was not my "soul" speaking in the essay. So, I began to plunk away at the keyboard with deliberate mechanical clarity.

My mind wandered and my imagination embraced my fingertips. With Machiavellian coldness, I typed nonstop for hours on my modest proposal for the 1990s. It developed into a horrible, detailed account of murder, imprisonment, and destruction of the human race. It is certainly disturbing to think just how easy it was for me to write this essay. On paper, my words actually appeared incredibly sincere, and the joke began to seem quite plausible, as if the author was presenting his true feelings on every page. I did not want the reader to brush it off as a mere joke, though. I wanted it to be engaging and to make the reader think at each point. When finished reading, the reader should realize that the proposal as a whole was anything but modest.

As for the proposal itself, it had two distinct parts. In the first part, I discussed the destruction of half the population of all races in the lower class. I continually used the wording "to better" to describe how I wanted to improve the situation of racism in America. I did not want to jump out and scream "Kill, kill, kill; imprison; slaughter; murder; destroy." In my essay, "better" had the same meaning as those harsh words, but it seemed a bit softer in its tone. I stated the following:

> The term "better" is quite ambiguous and can take on various meanings. I define "to better" as improving the overall society in any way possible. By "bettering" the conditions of a certain people within the society, we can contribute to the health of the nation. At the same time we can be directed towards a goal of racial harmony. In effect, I am asking for an extreme betterment, or extinguishing, of about fifty percent of the lower class population. (This immediately would help to alleviate the hunger issue.) As for the other fifty percent, a less extreme betterment should be made (for to better "extremely" this group as a whole would cause a loss in the valuable works and services they provide). They should be confined in various places across the nation and forced to provide services for the country and the persons within the country.

Upon finishing the first phase of the proposal, I proceeded to discuss the second phase's dynamics. In this phase, I proposed to drastically reduce differences between the ethnic groups. I wrote, unnerved at the horror I had conjured in my mind, and described the killing of ethnic groups as necessary to lessen racial differences. For instance, I observed the trait of skin color and proposed that all those with obvious skin color differences would be destroyed – dark and light. I read the list of people who would have to be "extremely bettered" in this manner. It read as follows:

> The following (ethnic groups or descendents of the groups named) would all need to be eradicated, or extremely bettered due to their skin colors being too dark or too light: Irish Americans, African-Americans, Asian-Americans, Jews, South Africans, Germans, Scandinavians, South Pacific Islanders, Caribbean Islanders, Hawaiian Islanders, Canadians, Vikings, Portuguese, Greeks, Middle Easterners, Turks, Russians, Eastern Europeans, Western Europeans, Alaskan Eskimos, Australians, and all from the continent of South America.

After I had written the list into the essay, I laughed. Tell me that you are not laughing at least a little. Tell me that this is not humorous. Isn't it obvious that no one would be left? I did think it was incredibly humorous, but perhaps a brash, white kid from New Jersey does not understand it all. I had little time to consider this; I was too caught up in the construct of the essay.

I finished the essay after this second phase, feeling

comfortable that I had achieved my goal (but not really knowing what the goal was). I smiled and added a comment of hope at the close of the essay, which I inserted in order to clarify that the essay was indeed a satire. After all, I still felt hope on the matter of racism. This close was remarkably easy for me to write, as was the whole paper. Looking back now, I realize that the paper did not really challenge me in any way. After all, it had been merely a joke to me.

The test came Tuesday morning, the day of the workshop with my professor and the other students. What would the others think of this proposal? Would they understand what I was trying to accomplish? Would they laugh? My uncertainty in the early morning melted as the sun rose, and I even walked up the stairs to the third floor workshop room with an air of confidence. I met the other students outside the room, and we all greeted each other. There was a moment of brief silence while we stood waiting for the workshop to begin. Mike broke the silence, looking up at me and saying, "You're crazy" (referring to my plan for killing various races). I agreed. After all, I had been out on a limb. Soon after Mike's comment, the workshop began. We all entered the room and took our seats (later I discovered that he refused to sit next to me because of the essay). We reviewed the other essays, analyzing and commenting on each work, until finally, we reached mine – the last one to be reviewed.

Mike was losing a battle with silence and could not hold back his emotions. "Wow!" he breathed. That was the most he could say of his true feelings about the paper though. After this, he basically stumbled with his words as he went through the motions of critiquing the work. He offered some encouragement, pointed out some sentence structure errors, but seemed altogether confused. He kept emphasizing that it seemed extremely radical.

I nodded in agreement, still feeling confident about the piece. Elizabeth followed Mike in the process. She also expressed some confusion. Then, she stated that my proposal had some faults and might not really solve racism.

Wait a minute. Not really solve racism? But it was not meant to be real. This was, in its essence, a joke – not real. They all did know it was a joke, right? "Hold on," I said, staring at the other students. "You all do realize this is a joke, right?" Following this statement, they all let out sighs of relief and smiled emphatically at me. The tension in the room, which I had not noticed until this point, dissipated quickly. They all relaxed and let down their guards, feeling safer that a sadist was not among them. Each student felt comfortable with me again and laughed at the misunderstanding.

Walking out of the workshop, I felt no such comfort. In fact, I was extremely agitated and uneasy. How had they missed the point? How did I not make it clear? The satire, the irony – it was all there in the paper. Still, each student had thought my words to be sincere. I shuddered as I walked towards the cafeteria. Strangely, the shuddering turned into bizarre laughter. And I kept on laughing, for the entire day. Even into the night I laughed – at myself, at their expressions of horror reading my paper, at the world in general.

The world? Has it gotten that bad? Has our world become so insane that the bizarre cannot be distinguished from the norm? Has racism itself become what we consider normal? I am not about to try to answer these questions. I can only imagine an outside observer looking down from the heavens and seeing the insanity of it all – burning crosses, church bombings, lynching. Surely, human beings should not consider this normal. Is it not bizarre? Furthermore, what would this outside observer think about the stories covered in the news headlines? We read the newspaper every day and become accustomed to it all. We think of the Holocaust as horrific and inconceivable, yet we sit and eat dinner in front of a news program describing the situation in Bosnia, or at least I have. In my essay, I described how I wanted to eradicate racism by "cleansing" America and destroying certain races. From my television set, I have seen the torture chambers in the former Bosnian hospital, the rotting corpses in the green fields alongside the road, and the blank expressions of the masses as they hobbled along the muddy paths in endless lines. This is the reality of ethnic cleansing, so similar to the "bettering" I had described in my proposal. This cannot be something normal, can it? And yet it exists in our world; it is reality. Are we living the satire?

The comments written in the margins from the professor and the students only seemed to confirm my fear that my proposal was not so far from reality as I had thought. Worst of all, some comments show how I was even naïve (isn't that a paradox – a naïve satirist?). I learned that my suggestions, in many cases, were not so original as I had believed. For example, the first phase of my proposal described the imprisonment of fifty percent of the lower class to provide services for the country. I read a comment beside this paragraph: "Is that not like the prison system?" I had not considered my idea as being similar to the prison system, but it was not long until I located information that confirmed the truth of this matter. An article entitled, "The Corporate Prison: The Production of Crime and the Sale of Discipline" by Karyl K. Kicenski states the following:

> Within the booming business of privatization, the benefits and popularity of "owning" prison labor are great. The privatization of prison institutions serves

as a contemporary illustration of the ends to which the "failure" of disciplining certain classes has successfully and functionally been put. The "failure" of the prison now pointedly and explicitly serves private corporate interests which transfers the handling of illegalities into their exploitation on behalf of profit. These profits are more than viable when inmates, who often earn between $.23 and $1.15 an hour, have as their only competition foreign-based labor (who in some ways are becoming more costly to utilize) who have been exploited by corporate entities for decades on the basis of some of the same advantages offered by prison inmates: a non-unionized work force, no minimum wage, no benefits, no healthcare, no Worker's Compensation, and finally, no commitment to employment longer than is advantageous to a clear profit margin.

Unknowingly, I had more or less described this privatization of prison systems and even the corporate benefits from the imprisonment of the lower class when I recommended the imprisonment of the lower class to get them out of the way.

And what about segregation and certain aspects of schooling? Aren't many people confined to certain areas merely to have them out of the way? In schools, the less capable are placed in rooms away from the others. Or worse, they are placed in special schools. I did not need to look too far for an example of this. My friend's brother basically had been forced to attend a special school because he did not meet the "academic standards" of the public school. And even when I was young, I remember waiting at the bus stop and laughing along with the other children as the "retard bus" passed, transporting the different children to the "retard school." These people have been essentially tossed aside and moved out of the way of the majority.

Likewise, segregation in the nation has confined certain ethnic groups, especially African-Americans, to ghettos, projects, backs of buses, etc. Yet those segregated (and those sent to special schools) still provide service for the nation. They are citizens, right? But "we the people" have separated those less capable in school. And "we the people" had written laws enforcing segregation of African-Americans until the late 1960s. This is the truth, not a satire.

This is a frightening fact for me, a sheltered boy from New Jersey. The words of the essay, in fact, are not a joke at all. In light of this, it is easy for me to understand how the other students misunderstood my essay. Many of the imaginative ideas I had suggested exist in our world. It was I who did not understand what I had written. I did not flinch when I wrote this cold, satirical piece. It did not frighten me then. But I am frightened now. The essay, the satire, is alive and real. I wrote it and read it feeling extremely comfortable that it was a good essay. Now, I read it, and my comfort level is shattered.

This is indeed a powerful thing – the truth, that is. And it is true that the bizarre is very real and present in our world. Any proposal I can think of may not be adequate when juxtaposed with the events of history. We have witnessed far more terrible proposals, and I fear what we may have to witness in the future.

I intended my essay to end with an emphasis on hope – to show that we must have hope in order to avoid resorting to proposals such as mine. But how could I discuss hope without really understanding the truth in the surrounding world? Hope without truth is for the comfortable. And the comfortable become complacent in their hopes. No, that type of hope is simple and easy to hold in your hands, but it is blind hope. I offer no such kind of optimism now as I did at the conclusion of my modest proposal. I have seen, and I admit to be scared. And maybe we all should see and be a little more afraid and a little less comfortable. Maybe it is what we do with this fear that can actually lead us to a better future. But what do I really know? For now, I'll keep hope in my pocket and truth by my side. And I'll pray for the day when someone may read my words and laugh at them, thinking of the essay as a joke – something inconceivable, unimaginable. It is not possible to read my essay as such now, though. Not now.

Pizza, Love and Other Sacrileges

Cristina Dacchille
Spring 2001 – Volume XXII

My first day of junior high, I fell in love. His name was Anthony. He had big brown eyes, adorable dimples and a smile that made me melt. That's all I really remember about him; or maybe that's all I ever knew. Regardless, I still thought about Anthony every night as I lay trying to fall asleep, about how cool he was and how cool I'd be if I were his girlfriend. All I wanted was for him to ask me out.

Surprising as it may be to some, the ever-popular Anthony never asked me (the class nerd) out (I know, I was shocked too). Instead, he asked out one of my best friends, and they went out for three weeks, which, to a seventh grader, is longer than forever! Well, anyway, they broke up, and five days later I fell in love with Ryan, the second most popular boy in my class. Eventually, though, Ryan asked out one of my best friends (the same one – I hated her!), and I discovered Todd.

And so the year went. I kept picking boys I wanted to go out with, and they kept passing over me for other girls. One day, I told my friend Jamie that, at this point in the year, I just wanted a boyfriend – I didn't care who he was.

That afternoon, Jamie was on the phone with Trish, and told her what I said. Trish went to the little league game that night and talked about it with Anthony.

Anthony told Lina, Lina told Ryan, and eventually, through some distorted link, Frankie Giordano found out.

Frankie Giordano was the boy who sat in the back of the classroom picking his nose. You know the one. There's one in every class. They are really sweet, smart, and interesting; but the fact remains that they pick their nose. And that makes them completely undatable. So when Frankie asked me out that night on the phone, it should surprise no one that I said no. I mean, come on – even I have standards.

Unfortunately, I didn't choose my words of rejection very tactfully. I crushed the poor kid. He spent an hour on the phone with me, crying and saying, "But Cristina – I really love you!" Since I did not have a response to this completely unexpected emotional outburst, I did what any self-respecting thirteen-year-old would have done – I hung up, not sure if the sound I heard was the click of the phone hanging up or the shatter of Frankie's heart breaking.

Some of you (especially the men among you) may be rolling your eyes at the moment, knowing full well that this is going to be one of those essays about first kisses and unrequited love and rejection. Guess again, boys (and you too, ladies!). No, I told you this story for one reason and one reason only: to demonstrate to you the way people so commonly abuse the word love. Have you ever noticed that any time people like something, even just a little bit, they feel the need to say they love it? "I loved that movie!" "Ohmygod, I am in love with that dress!" "I love the smell of white-out and permanent markers." Well, okay, maybe that last one is just me; but you get my point. People take the word love lightly. Once a word reserved for personal relationships and strong feelings of the heart ("How do I love thee, let me count the ways…"), love has become a word most commonly used to describe the way we feel towards pizza and chocolate ice cream.

While there is nothing wrong with pizza love in and of itself, it is my belief that if the object of your affection is incapable of caring for you back (such as the slice with pepperoni and mushrooms), then what you're feeling is not love. Then again, even if the object of your affection *is* capable of loving you back, it might still not be love. I mean, how many times a day do you say "I love you" to someone? I know I do it constantly, and so do the people around me.

Last Saturday night, I was at a party with some friends. People who had a large supply of, *ahem*, alcoholic beverages were throwing this particular gathering. Many of the guests present were consuming large amounts of these beverages (except me, of course), and a number of them were becoming quite intoxicated. One boy came up to me, looked me deep in the eyes, and said, "Katie, I love you." Then he puked all over my shoes. Now, my name is not Katie, number one. Number two, well, he vomited. I'm guessing on the basis of these two clues that his love for me wasn't exactly soul consuming.

Situations like these don't surprise many people. And yet, something deep down inside of us tells us that they should probably shock us out of our own skin. "I love you" isn't a phrase that should be used on just anybody...or is it? The answer to this question depends on what your definition of love is. If you're still in a junior high mentality, and to you, love is simply admiring big brown eyes and melting under the heat of a warm smile, then sure, it's okay to use it whenever you feel like it. Use it on your mom, your dad, your friends, your teacher – hell, use it on the mailman, it doesn't matter. If, however, you've grown in your understanding of the heart, and you believe (as I do) that love goes deeper than that, then maybe you should think twice before you tell the fry guy at McDonald's how much you love him just because of his cool skull and crossbones tattoo.

If you're going to start taking those three little words more seriously, it's important to understand what you mean when you say them. In other words, you have to define love. Sound impossible? It's not; but it is rather broad. Every corner you turn, every web page you click on and every book that you open has its own definition of love. So which one is right? That, my friend, is something you have to decide for yourself. Whether it comes from someone else or from you does not matter – what matters is that you believe in it.

My definition of love is not my own. It comes from the writer/philosopher Plato, and can be found in the dialogue, the *Symposium*. In the *Symposium*, several different men discuss (you guessed it) love. One of the speakers in the dialogue, Aristophanes, describes love through a myth. He says that when the gods first created human beings, they were created in such a way that each body was actually composed of two people, a male and a female. For reasons too long to discuss here, the gods decided that this was a bad idea, and sawed each person in half, creating two bodies from one soul, and leaving both bodies, male and female, in need of completion.

Aristophanes goes on to say that each person spends his entire life attempting to complete himself through his relationships with others. When finally the person stumbles upon "his other half," he is complete; he is in love. Love, therefore, is reserved for one person and is most extraordinary and unique in nature. Much like a fingerprint or a DNA sample, Aristophanes believed that whom you love identified quite precisely who you are.

I am aware that this definition of love is narrow. It applies only to romantic love, between a man and a woman, and it allows only for a person to have one "true" love in his lifetime. While these restrictions are certainly in need of correction (what about love between two friends? Or a mother and a daughter? Or a person and his God?), it is a beautiful story, and a good definition when attempting to explain the sacredness of the words "I love you."

The other definition of love that I tend to use is by Alexander Smith, and is a bit broader in its interpretation. Smith defines love as "the discovery of ourselves in another, and the delight in that recognition." For me, this definition takes Aristophanes' explanation and brings it a step further. In Aristophanes' definition, love is the completion of yourself in another person. In Smith's, it is the finding of yourself in another person and the joy of that discovery. The two combine very easily to form my own definition of love. That is, recognizing in someone else a quality you yourself lack, and through that recognition, maturing and growing into that quality yourself; *or*, discovering in someone else a quality that you yourself have and never appreciated, and, through that discovery, increasing your own self-knowledge.

No matter which part of my definition you use, love is not just some feeling floating around up there in the air. It is not all pink hearts and flowers, nor does it have anything to do with pizza. Love is real. It is not easy, nor is it always fun. In fact, sometimes, love can be downright nitty-gritty and hard to deal with.

My mother and I have always had a hard time getting along. I love her to death, but when I was little, I used to think she was out of her mind. Really. I thought that one day, men in white jackets were going to come to our house and take her away. This thought was especially prominent in my mind while driving with her.

You see, my mom would always have the radio on in

the car when she drove my little brothers and me back and forth to school. She kept the radio on really low; that is, until one of her favorite songs came on. Then she would turn it up so loud the doors would shake. I would have been fine if the songs were "cool" (and by that I mean Paula Abdul or New Kids on the Block, or whatever it was I thought was so great during the late '80s and early '90s). But it wasn't cool. It was 101.1 CBS FM – the oldies station. It was mortifying. I would slouch down in the seat and cover my eyes, hoping no one would see me, that no one would know that the lunatic driving the station wagon was (gulp) my mother.

When my mom saw me do that, her playful nature would not just let me lay down and die in peace. No, that's when she started making the car dance. Yes, I said dance. She would take this route where there were never any other cars, and make the car do these little swerves. Then she'd yell back at me that the car was dancing, that I should be dancing too. I just slumped further down in my seat and prayed we would get home soon, before anyone saw me in this nut-mobile.

Most people would not think that this story has anything to do with love. I, however, disagree. In fact, to me, this is the perfect example of love as a force of self-recognition and appreciation. How, do you ask? Relax, I'm getting there (remember: "Love is patient...").

A few weeks ago I went home for a weekend to see one of my little brother's big soccer games. The game was forty minutes away from my house, and I did not want to drive there alone. So, I piled my other little brother and my boyfriend into our family car (now a minivan), and started out on what ended up being a very long trip. We got caught in an hour's worth of traffic. Frustrated, I began flipping through the radio stations. I passed 101.1 FM quickly, only to go back after hearing a snippet of "It's Still

Rock and Roll to Me." I love that song. A smile immediately flew onto my face. I turned the radio on as loud as it would go, and began singing and dancing at the top of my lungs. After about a minute of that, I looked over to see my boyfriend and my brother sinking lower and lower in their seats. Puzzled, I began to try to make them smile too. Without even realizing what I was doing, I made the car dance, using the brakes to match the beat of the song. They still thought I was out of my mind, and soon I forgot about them. I was happy and I was having fun. Most importantly, I was making the most out of a difficult situation, something that my far too serious eighteen-going-on-fifty personality is almost never able to do.

Hours later, safely situated on my couch, far away from New Jersey rush hour hell, I remembered my childhood driving experiences with my mother. Looking back, I realized that my mom was not crazy; she was just trying to be herself, something that in recent years I have grown to appreciate about her. Her playfulness, her carefree attitude and her young-at-heart spirit are all qualities that play a part in my love for her. And through this love, I was finally able to recognize a part of me that was lacking in development: my playful side, my ability to have fun doing anything. I saw it alive and in color through her actions, and no matter how crazy they seemed to me at the time, I recognized them later as qualities I wanted, and in fact needed to have. I grew. I changed. And I enjoyed every minute of it.

That, to me, is love. Finding missing parts of yourself in someone else. Appreciating who you are because of the people you love. Growing. Maturing. Changing. And that definition, unlike Aristophanes', fits almost every kind of love. With this definition, it is possible to love anyone: family, friends, and the poverty-stricken alike.

My friend Maria used to work at a soup kitchen

near my house. One night we got into one of those deep philosophical conversations, and she admitted to me that she never knew who she was before she began working there. I asked her how that could be; I mean, how do you not know who you are? And she answered something to the effect of, "Cristina, all my life I have defined myself by the things I have: what clothes I wear, what CDs I listen to, what makeup I use. Meeting people who have nothing changed that because they still, despite their poverty, know who they are. And to me, that means I must not know who I am. Because right now, if everything I had suddenly got taken away from me, I wouldn't think very highly of myself."

Now, most people wouldn't say that Maria "loved" the people at the shelter, but I would like to argue that she *did* love them. She recognized something in them that she herself lacked: self-knowledge. And because of that recognition, she was motivated to dig deeper until she discovered just who she was. That is a form of love. That is just as sacred and inspirational as the love between a mother and a daughter: it is love between a person and her fellow man.

Another type of love that is commonly overlooked is the love of a higher being. I myself am Catholic. I believe that there is a God, and that He is up there somewhere, watching all that I do, and even aiding me in my journey through life. I also believe that this God loves me. Why? Because He created me in His image. He sees me in all sorts of great qualities, and enjoys seeing me use them for His good. His love is parental in its nature.

Many people who have strong spiritual beliefs use the word "love" to describe how they feel about their God or how their God feels about them. This isn't wrong because it is something they believe deeply in. They are not just flippantly using the word; they mean it. And that's all that matters. Anyone who believes that what they are feeling is indeed love cannot be wrong. The problem comes when people who don't genuinely mean it use the word on people who do. That is a dangerous situation, one in which both people end up getting hurt. That's what happened with Chris and me.

I met Chris on a retreat that I went on a few years back. He was having a lot of problems, and I spent much of my weekend just talking with him. We spent that entire weekend together, comfortable in our new friendship and each happy to have found a confidant. When the retreat was over, and we returned home, we continued to talk to each other and grow in our friendship. Eventually, as happens with many boy-girl friendships, we both started to become attracted to each other. For the first month or two, I was in heaven. I had a boyfriend who was not only funny and cute and attractive, but who was also one of my closest friends. I thought that life couldn't get any better. Then the inevitable happened. He said it.

We were on the phone, talking about nothing at all, when all of a sudden, out of the blue, he blurted it out.

"I love you."

"What?"

"I love you."

I twisted the phone cord nervously. The moment of truth. Would I be able to stick to my own principles? Would I say it, even though I didn't mean it? What would happen if I said it? Worse, what would happen if I didn't? He'll think I don't like him, and I do.

"I love you too."

And with those four little words, I ruined a great friendship. Because eventually, Chris realized that I didn't love him. My feelings, while wonderful, were just not that strong. He was not "my other half" and I knew it. And so did he. And the day he realized it was the day he broke up with me, and the last day I spoke to him. He was hurt, angry, and feeling incredibly embarrassed and humiliated. I don't blame him for not wanting to talk to me. I blame myself and my inability to be honest about my feelings and to think before using words so powerful when I didn't mean them.

The words "I love you" are three of the most dangerous words in the English language. Playing around with them when discussing food, hobbies, and other frivolities is, in a way, irreverent because, by doing so, you are showing that you have no respect for the sacredness of love. Then again, saying them when you don't mean them, like I did with Chris, shows that you don't have the courage to really use the words correctly.

We all use and abuse the word love daily. I'm not saying that this is the worst thing anyone could have ever done. I'm not even saying that it is an easy habit to break. What I am saying is that I believe in love between two people – true love, without pepperoni or anything. And my beliefs are so strong that I try not to abuse the phrase "I love you." Through the vastness of the English language, the feat is actually possible. There are the words "like" and "care about," "lust" and "passion," "worship" and "adore," "compassion" and "understanding." With so many words to choose from, there is no need to say "love" that often. By using alternative expressions, you restrict love, giving it a certain level of importance. Kind of like that good silverware your mom has. Your mom would kill you if you ever tried to fool around with it. Why? Because it's worth its weight in sterling, it's more important to her than her own arm, and (to your mother) it's more sacred than holy water on Easter Sunday. You would never use it on any old Monday. You would never use it with just any old people. And, most importantly, you would never use it for any old pizza.

Plop!

Peter Blair

Spring 2001 – Volume XXII

> "This is the substance of our Plot-
> For those who play the Perfect Shot,
> There are ten thousand who do not."
> *–Grantland Rice[1]*

"Foooooore!" The echo of my voice can be heard through the green fairways of Stone E. Lea Country Club as my ball lands on the wrong green.

"Oh well…there's always next hole," shouts my partner Murph, whose ball is lying 250 yards away in the center of the first fairway.

"Easy for you to say," I can tell that it's going to be a long day.

As we walk away from the tee and I walk through the woods to find my ball, I begin to think. Why exactly do I love golf so much? I'm really not very good. I've been playing for seven years now, and I have yet to show any drastic signs of improvement. It's looking now like I never will. I'm starting to lose hope. But, I'm still out here, and it's certainly not the $25 green fees every single time I want to play a round.

I look through the dark green rows of pine and oak at Murph, who is smiling from ear to ear. "I'd like to wipe that smile right off his face," I think as I find my ball on the next fairway and line up to hit my shot. I pull the club back and swing as hard as I can only to have the ball skim 100 yards along the ground, bounce off a rock, and land smack in the center of the green. Just as I planned I look over and see Murph laughing hysterically.

"Hey, no one's taking pictures!" I shout.

"You should be thankful no one's taking pictures," he calls back.

I finally hit a shot with a good result, and it looks anything but pretty. I'm certainly no Tiger Woods, but I'm still out here; I'm still trying. Again I ask myself, "Why?"

Most of my friends think golf is pointless. They tell me that it's a waste of energy. My friend Alex says, "It's stupid. Such a waste of time. You spend three hours of the day walking around, bullshitting, and about fifteen minutes actually hitting a golf ball. And it costs an arm and a leg. Stupid. Stupid. Stupid." Alex used to be a golfer himself. He wasn't very good either; I suspect that's why he feels this way. Popular comedian George Carlin once said, "Watching golf is about as exciting as watching two flies have sex." He's obviously not a golfer. A golfer would realize that there's more to golf than the simple art of hitting the golf ball and more than merely walking around a golf course for three hours. Golf is about fellowship and camaraderie and building relationships.

According to my dad, "Nothing beats taking a day off from work to hit the golf course with your friends. We always seem to learn new things about each other and the winner always buys everyone a round of drinks." According to author John Updike, "Golf expresses the man, as every weekend foursome knows."[2] They are both right: golf can teach us a lot about each other and about ourselves. Even though Murph may be my opponent and, on the outside, I'm rooting against him, something inside of me still feels happy for him when he succeeds. We can't look at golf as being a battle between the two of us, because ultimately we both have the same goal: not conquering each other, but conquering the golf course itself.

Conquering the golf course requires creativity. I can't even begin to tell how many times my ball had been stuck against a tree, or under a branch, or buried in a bunker, with almost no hopes of hitting a great shot. But I've never given up or picked my ball up. I've always used my imagination to create a shot that would meet my needs. Golf has helped me realize that I can be creative. I remember a few years ago, when I was out on this same golf course. My ball was lying right up against a tree, right where my body would ordinarily be to hit the shot. Instead of pitching out or dropping the ball away from the tree, I pondered for a moment, and picked up my putter. I stood on the opposite side of the ball, as though I were left-handed. I pulled back and – and using the backhand side of the putter – forced the ball about 80 yards up the fairway, just short of the hole.

Now I've finally reached the green. I'm here in two shots and this is Par 4, so I have two putts to try to make par. I notice that my ball is lying only 20 feet away from the hole, so I try to take my time. I bend down, line up my putt, and concentrate. I visualize the ball falling right into the bottom of the hole, and I imagine the plop I will hear as it falls in. I stand over the ball, watching it intently. I pull the putter back slowly, pause, and swing at the ball harder than I had planned, sending the ball rolling another 20 feet past the hole.

"Son of a – " I begin to scream.

"Shh!" Murph reminds me to keep quiet.

"Why?" I ask him, "Why me?"

"Don't worry. We've got 17 more holes to play," he replies. "Don't get yourself upset now."

As I step back to gather myself, Murph steps up to make his putt. His ball is lying about five feet from the hole in perfect position. With seemingly no effort, he steps right up to the ball and knocks it into the hole. I hear it strike the bottom! "Plop!" That was supposed to be my sound. Instead, now I am struggling to make par. If I miss this shot, I won't be able to let myself live it down. There is no worse feeling than the discontent of working hard only to have your goal elude you. At the same time, playing well is rewarding because there is nothing better than the feeling of accomplishment after knocking a shot in the hole.

I step up once again, concentrate, and strike the ball beautifully. The ball rolls right toward the hole. I'm starting to get excited. With a smile on my face, I pump my fists in the air. The ball approaches the hole. Two feet away. One foot away. The ball hits the lip of the hole and bounces out. My spirits drop.

"That's not fair," I whisper to Murph, being careful not to get too loud this time.

"No one ever said golf is supposed to be fair," he says.

"Look at you, with your words of wisdom," I mutter facetiously.

> When drives are all hole-high and straight,
> And every yarn we tell is true,
> Golf will be wearisome and flat,
> When there is naught to grumble at.
> – *Thomas Risk*[3]

We've been on the course for about fifteen minutes now, and we've done nothing but argue and grumble. I've never had so much fun with Murph though. There's nothing like a great argument on the golf course. It helps to get the frustration out of our systems. It helps us keep ourselves from going crazy about the game, and it adds a little excitement at the same time. Both of us know that when the day is over, we'll each go home and forget about it completely. This is what separates golf from other sports in my opinion. Golf may not have the flashy brawls of hockey or the wild head-to-head battles of football, but it does have its own unique squabbles found within the quiet competition of a day on the golf course. These squabbles are different because at the end of the day, usually no one can even remember what they were about. But during the round, they help relieve stress and keep everyone relaxed.

All of these aspects of golf could tell us why, according to Alec Morrison, over half of all middle-aged American men play golf today, compared to a mere 15% in 1975[4]. There has to be something that has drawn all these people to the sport in the past few years. Has it been the camaraderie? Has it been the dominant professional golfers – Jack Nicklaus, Tom Watson, and Tiger Woods – over the past three decades who have influenced and inspired them to take up the game? Has it been the fact that golf gives them the chance to relax and withdraw themselves from the busy rigors of everyday life?

Most likely, it's been a combination of all of these things. I started to play golf seven years ago because I needed something to do. I've stuck with it because I have fun playing it. I've learned so much about myself from playing golf. For instance, I've learned that I'm really creative, and even when I'm not good at something, I don't have to quit doing it. Just as I don't count myself out when I'm faced with a problem in life.

I've also noticed that golf brings people of all different backgrounds and abilities together. Anyone, of any ability, gender, or background can play golf. Just last year, a blind man got a hole-in-one on a Par 3. Nothing stopped him from playing golf, and nothing should stop me either. Inspirational stories like this one encourage me to stay out on the course and to keep trying, never giving up. Even if I'm not the strongest or most talented golfer on the course, I still get out there. And even though sometimes I get frustrated, golf keeps me humble. Golf shows that I can do something even when I'm not the best, and I can still enjoy doing it.

Well, now I am faced with a short two-foot putt to salvage my 5 on this hole. I've looked it over for about a minute, and I feel pretty confident about this one. I step right up to it, line the club up, pull back, and putt. "PLOP!" There it is! The sweetest sound to any golfer. That sound – the sound all golfers love to hear – that's what keeps me out here; that's what keeps me trying. Just because it took Murph three strokes to hear his "Plop!" and it took me five to hear mine doesn't mean that mine is worth any less. In fact, to me, it's worth more. It proves I can do it. Hearing my "Plop!" proves that I have accomplished my goal. My dad agrees with me. "Golf really wouldn't be the same if the ball went into the hole silently," he says. The more I think about it, the more I realize how true it is. A baseball player hears the "crack" of the ball hitting the bat; a basketball player hears the "swoosh" of the net as his ball goes through the hoop. Golf is no different. The sound we hear represents the same feeling of accomplishment that other athletes feel when they succeed at what they're trying to do.

Now I know for sure why people golf: they golf for that sound. Not just the sound, but everything that's behind it: the fellowship, the accomplishment, the pride, and adrenaline that all originate in the one sweet simple sound. I guess now I know why George Carlin and so many others hate golf then. They haven't heard the sound. They haven't stood there, with golf club in hands, eyes fixed on the hole, hearts pounding in their chests, ears ringing with the harmonious "Plop." The feeling never gets old. Every time I hear the sound, I feel just as fulfilled and excited as the time before. I wish that everybody in the world could hear this sound for themselves just one time, and then maybe they could see what they're missing out on. Until then, I feel like I'm in on a secret, because I get to hear the heavenly sound 18 times every time I step out onto a golf course. It is clear to me that golfers are truly blessed in a way that only they can understand and appreciate.

"Ready?" Murph snaps me out of my daze.

"Of course. We've still got 17 holes to play," I respond.

"Well, then, what are you waiting for?" he asks.

I smile at him, realizing once again how lucky I am to be out here, pick up my bag, and walk silently toward the second tee. My ears are still ringing.

Works Cited

[1] Rice, Grantland. "Dedicated to the Duffer." The Impossible Art of Golf. Ed. Alec Morrison. Oxford: Oxford University Press, 1994.

[2] Updike, John. "Sam Snead and Arnold Palmer." The Impossible Art of Golf. Ed. Alec Morrison. Oxford: Oxford University Press, 1994.

[3] Risk, Thomas. "The Golfer's Discontent." The Impossible Art of Golf. Ed. Alec Morrison. Oxford: Oxford University Press, 1994.

[4] Morrison, Alec. "Introduction." The Impossible Art of Golf. Ed. Alec Morrison Oxford: Oxford University Press, 1994.

A Bittersweet Journey

Jennifer Casey
Spring 2001 – Volume XXII

What do I want to be when I grow up? Ordinary. Stereotypical. I don't want to be a princess or an actress. I want to be something normal. Maybe a teacher. I am six years old, biting my lip as I concentrate to maneuver my absurdly thick pencil about my writing tablet. My desk mate, my best friend Jason, tells one of the other boys that he's going to be a baseball player for the Orioles someday. I want to tell him he is wrong, but my teacher says no talking during seatwork.

Mrs. O'Connor corrects papers at the front of the classroom and glances around to hush the noisy kids. As she returns to her grading, I watch her red pen move rhythmically around a paper, then onto another. This repeated action appeals to me with its methodical typicality.

I am only a child, but I have already given up the lofty ambitions my other classmates cling to. I don't yet know why I don't want to be an athlete or a superstar. I just know that most people don't do that, and that's a good enough reason for me. I want to be like Mrs. O'Connor. Not until I reach my sophomore year of high school will I understand teaching as something more than a routine, mechanical job. For now, I strive to embody conventionality, and I still have much growing to do before I can appreciate the value of individuality.

My eyes burn with tears as I sit on a cold examination table at Johns Hopkins Hospital, listening to an ear-reconstruction specialist explain surgical procedures to my parents. I am ten years old, and I don't understand what he is saying.

"Jennifer will need to see Dr. Bert Brent at *The Ear Institute* in California. He is a world-renowned specialist who has performed various operations..." He speaks to my mother and father as though I'm not even in the room.

"California!" I exclaim. "Mom, I *cannot* miss school to go all the way to California to have my dumb ear fixed." But my mother silences me with a look and my father continues to nod at the doctor's words. They listen to him as though he actually says something intriguing. I feel hurt and completely alone in this cold, sterile room. My right hand reaches up to shield the ear that is the subject of this awful meeting. I feel the soft flesh and shudder to think that someone is going to change it. Affectionately calling my right ear my "little ear" for some time now, I've grown accustomed to its smallness and its seashell-like inward curl.

In their concern for my well-being, my parents have decided that I will undergo surgery to correct this deformity. I hate them for this. None of the other kids at school have to give up their Saturday mornings to sit in a doctor's office, facing the reality of an abnormal appearance. My eyes close, and I see Sally at her horseback-riding lesson, Rachael and Sara, in their black leotards and pink slippers, giggling in the church basement during their ballet lesson. My friends don't have to sit here, in a dull examination room because, unlike me, they all look normal.

I don't like having a deformity, but I am used to it,

and I have learned to conceal it. Unlike the other girls in my fourth grade class, I don't wear my hair in ponytails or braids, and I don't have piercings to display cute token earrings. My long thick hair trails down my neck, day after day, covering my ears. I long to pull it away from my face, but I don't. I cannot forget that boy's hurtful comments from years ago, and I keep my ear hidden so that no one can make fun of me ever again.

My preschool teacher, Miss Doris, says it's time to go outside, and we, the "butterfly group," grab our jackets and hurry to the playground. Miss Doris retreats to the bench to converse with the other teachers, and I am left alone with my classmates. We play our usual games of tag and hide-and-seek, but today is different. Kyle, a mean, nosy little boy, notices my ear.

"What's wrong with your ear?" he cries out. I don't know how to respond.

"Come on. Answer me. Why does it look different?" He comes closer to me. "I said, 'Why does it look different?'" I don't answer him because I don't know what to say. I have never thought of my ear as different before. But today, I am mortified. For the first time, I realize I am abnormal.

Later, at our preschool graduation, we recite a poem.

"I know numbers, I know shapes, I know that purple stands for grapes," I repeat in a singsong that blends with the other four-year-old voices. Everyone smiles, excited to stand on the stage, but I feel insecure under my lopsided grin. I've learned more than numbers and shapes in school; I've learned that it isn't any fun to be different.

As my reconstruction surgery date approaches, I don't hate the idea as much. After my deformity is corrected, I won't feel as insecure anymore. I step timidly into my science teacher's classroom, and through her window, I can see my classmates chasing a ball on the soccer field.

"May I talk to you for a minute, Ms. Madeline?" I ask.

"Of course, Jennifer." She smiles at me. "What do you need?"

"I just wanted to remind you that Friday is my last day. I will be out for two weeks because of my surgery." My face reddens as I call attention to my flawed ear.

"I'll have your assignments ready on Friday morning," she says softly. I thank her and leave to remind my other teachers of my upcoming absence. They receive me kindly, promising to have my assignments ready, but I still feel humiliated. As I return to my classroom, the other kids enter the building.

Sally walks in, tucks her long blonde hair behind her ears, and calls, "Hey Jen. Where were you? You missed a great game."

"I had to talk to some of the teachers," I say, looking down at the linoleum floor. The other girls approach to share gossip with us. I smile as Rachael and Sara take turns telling me about the fight on the playground. Their story is not particularly funny, but I smile because I know that soon I won't be different anymore.

"Rachael, it's ninety degrees outside today. Why are you dressed like that?" I ask one of my closest friends. The girl who only last year wore pastel dresses and ribbon-tied ponytails stands before me in a long-sleeved black shirt and thick, heavy combat boots. She scowls and ignores my question.

On this warm August day, I am dismayed with the friends with whom I reunite at my sophomore orientation session. They haven't changed since June. They've decided that it's time to adopt Thoreau's ideas and "march to the beat of their own drummers." I am baffled. I have watched these girls habitually since kindergarten, and I can't understand why they now want to set themselves apart from everyone else. Sally and Sara have darkened their sunny hair and Rachael has cropped her long, flowing curls. They have abandoned colorful clothing for apparel of the darkest hue. Color is out, black is in. Blackness – darkness – is the absence of light, and light is certainly now lacking in their lives. They skip pep rallies to write haunting poetry, and they despise the popular crowd because of their conformity.

I am torn. I have worked for years to achieve normality, and now my friends are shedding the type of shell that I have labored so hard to create. As I survey my newly changing friends, I am transported back to that cold examination room from years before. Once again, I am alone and defeated in my quest for normality. Almost five years have passed since my reconstruction surgery, and I no longer view my ear as an abnormality. But now I face a new obstacle – maintaining my sense of normality amid my friends' newfound identities. Although they are beginning to define themselves as individuals, I have not yet realized the beauty in individuality.

On Sunday, the first of August, I stand in my bedroom trembling as hot tears roll down my cheeks. Diagnosed with uterine cancer five months ago, my mother has endured hellish radiation and chemotherapy treatments throughout the summer. Now she is dying in the next room, and my heart is breaking. I can't bear to imagine life without her, but my twelve-year-old mind cries, "Things like this don't happen to people my age. Why is this happening to me?" I despise myself for being so egocentric, but I am in an awkward adolescent stage where it's hard enough to maintain any sense of self-assurance, let alone endure a major calamity.

Rachael is an altar server at the funeral mass, but I cannot bear to look at her. I stare ahead at the grainy wooden pew, hearing the priest droning faintly in the background. Looking past Father Callahan, I count the bleeding hearts on the wallpaper behind him. My eyes trace the outline of the white marble altar. I glance at the stained-glass windows, scowl at rejoicing angels and panes inscribed with words like "peace" and "hope," and turn away. Looking down at the rack of hymnals, I see the same blue books I used when I attended elementary school masses here. I think of my first-grade prayer partner and of my favorite church songs. I think of everything except the fact that my mother has just died. I cannot yet abandon the illusion that I am a member of a typical family.

To celebrate my best friend Sara's seventeenth birthday, my closest friends and I gather at Chi-Chi's. We munch tortilla chips with salsa and chat idly. Our conversation centers on Sally's new boyfriend, and, being ever so modest, she turns the discussion to college, which gradually leads to vague speculations about careers and marriage and the four of us living together when we're old ladies.

Sara, always wondering about her future, asks, "You guys, what should I be when I grow up?" We avoid each other's glances, and an awkward silence looms over our table for a moment.

"Well," Sara says with a sigh, "what about you Jen?" I don't hesitate because I feel quite certain about my future.

"I want to be the epitome of stereotypical normality. I think I want to be a – " Rachael's silverware clatters to the floor, and other restaurant patrons stare as she bends to pick up the utensils.

"Uh, here they are," she says. "Sometimes, I just don't understand you, Jen." I am somewhat taken aback by her comment because she is the one individual who amazes me with her eccentricity and uniqueness. Nevertheless, I don't really care what my friends think, because right now, I still crave normality.

"Here is your assignment."

"Thanks," I reply, uninterestedly flipping through the lab manual my Advanced Placement Biology teacher had handed me. It is mid-fall of my senior year, and I have enough to worry about with college applications and three other Advanced Placement classes that I can't think about biology right now. I abandon my assignment to converse with my lab partner, Erica, the embodiment of normality that I have somehow come to despise. She shares a story about last night's family dinner. Uttering a half-laugh, I say, "Oh, that's interesting. I skipped dinner last night to study history."

"Oh. My parents don't allow me to skip dinner, even when I am not hungry," she replies. For some reason, I feel the need to explain myself to her.

"Well, I used to eat with my father and my step-mother. But last year I gave up meat during Lent, and they eat meat almost every night, so I'm not really into family dinners anymore."

"You know what, Jen?" she starts. "All of the things you say... I'm really glad I'm not you."

Images of my conflicts with normality race through my head. I feel the tiny soft flesh of my "little ear." I hear my friends droning on about the importance of not following the crowd. I see my blank face at my mother's funeral. But I remember both the incredible insight that has accompanied each adversity and the self-confidence that I have gained over the past few years. When I graduate later in the year, I will articulate more clearly my transformation from an insecure young girl to a self-assured young woman.

My voice shakes as I deliver a speech to the many people crowded into St. Joseph's Monastery for Baccalaureate Mass. I have earned the honor of valedictorian, and I share with my fellow graduates, not a typical farewell speech, but a personal anecdote.

My words honor my sophomore English teacher, Margaret Kenney, the woman whose confidence in my abilities has allowed me to find my own self-confidence. As I speak, I remember my older sister's words after hearing an early version of my speech. She had recalled that only our mother had ever instilled the same sense of confidence in her that Mrs. Kenney has implanted in me. I smile, grateful that I have experienced this motherly gift, despite the loss of my own mother. I once envisioned teaching as an ordinary profession, but having experienced firsthand a teacher's extraordinary ability to change a student's life, I now view the vocation differently. Traveling far from the child who deserted lofty dreams for normality, I have begun to dream of remarkable possibilities for my future.

Erica stares at me, waiting for a reply to her comment. I return her gaze and smile.

"You know what? That's really great, but the funny thing is, I would really hate to be anyone but me."

Art of Living: Give and Take

Bailey E. Borzecki
Fall 2005 – Volume XXVI

> "That the sea-wave, as it surges with complex eddies, flowing and ebbing, should fit with such perfect adjustment to the rock-surface of the cliff is one of the most inevitable of natural things, so inevitable and so natural, that it would seem foolish to question why or how such close reciprocal adjustment is accomplished."
>
> – *E.L. Grant Watson*

Closing the door of my car, I let out a sigh of hot air. The white steam evaporated against the dark night air, and I started to walk towards my apartment. Another late weekend night, another similar ending, another day on the calendar to cross off. It seems that, once you get into a routine, days overlap and you can't distinguish between this Friday and that Saturday. I shivered as my sandals splashed through the small remaining puddles on the asphalt, displacing the water into tiny drops. A bluish glow seemed to emanate from the droplets. They were reflecting light. I looked up, awkwardly tilting my head skywards. My breath caught as I realized where the light was coming from. The sky resembled navy-colored satin; its richness almost seemed tactile. Stars bigger and brighter than any I had seen hung precisely in the clear air.

Several storms had passed through earlier during the afternoon, taking every cloud in the sky and leaving wet grass. I looked up and thought I could see past the stars and deeper into the night than I had ever seen before. I sat down on the cold sidewalk and rested on my elbows, just watching. The cold smelled like the woody smoke of a campfire and I could feel the seasons change right there. I could feel the leaves drying and changing color, falling like the rain that had soaked the earth that afternoon. The scent of the air was like a photograph that is lost but resurfaces unexpectedly, a reminder of a past moment and a glimpse into what will eventually come to be.

I looked down at my frozen toes and at my left foot. The familiar blue pattern glowed under the light of the stars. Four bigger stars with seven points and one smaller one tucked in between with five points. The five brightest stars of the constellation "Southern Cross" are found in the southern hemisphere, though in the northern hemisphere they are tattooed in fading blue ink on the top of my numb foot. I wiggled my toes, hoping to get the blood flowing back. The rain started to fall around me, and I closed my eyes and breathed in.

The weather was almost identical the day we drove along the Great Ocean Road in August 2003. I never thought I would spend my twentieth birthday in Australia, but there I was, starting my twentieth year on Earth in a place I wouldn't have expected to be. The Australian sky was a thick layer of dull gray, and it would open up every now and then and shed some water weight. We rode on a bus for about three hours, around cliffs jutting out over the agitated ocean that smashed methodically against the beaches. Mostly everyone slept, but I kept a small meteorologist-like eye on the intervals of rain. The slick roads were threatening, especially around the tight curves up along the coast, so my chest would tighten every time the rain grew heavier.

The bus stopped on one side of a highway, and we ate peanut butter and jelly sandwiches. The guide then simply pointed in the direction across the highway and we started to walk. And then it was one of those moments that you think will never happen, but the gray slabs of nebulous started to move and open up, and a sky crept out that was the most perfect shade of blue. The clouds that framed it were as white as snow, and I felt like I was looking at a photograph that had been altered, because I didn't think nature really allowed for this kind of flawlessness.

We reached the other side of the highway and approached the edge of one of the viewing lookout points. I stepped cautiously, conscious of slipping and crashing over the cliff to a bloody death. I looked out and saw sand-colored stone giants. Stone giants just wading in the surf. They were separate from the huge cliff we were standing on. Twelve of them lined the coast as I looked to my left and right. Each one was distinct and different from the others, but they all stood tall and powerful. The waves crashed into them, flowed around their edges and settled into foam on the beach. For about one hundred meters out, past the rocks, the water was bubbling and white, steaming and churning, recycling itself as the tide arrived and retreated. The water past the rocks was a deep turquoise, but not the kind of turquoise you'd expect to see in the Caribbean or somewhere tropical. Unique to its location, it was Great Ocean Road-turquoise. The color of the water and the sky touched at some points where the clouds left gaps, and they blended so that you couldn't tell where the water began and the sky ended.

I finally realized I hadn't breathed for quite some time, so I let out the air I had been holding in my chest and then deeply inhaled the salty, rainy air. The cold was so poignant that it felt like it was winter. I stood at various viewing points for hours, just watching the waves build up, crash into the rock and recede back again. The waves were responsible for the twelve stones, or Twelve Apostles, as most people recognize them. The Apostles had their beginnings up to 20 million years ago with the forces of nature attacking the soft limestone of the Port Campbell cliffs. The limestone was created through the build up of skeletons of marine creatures on the sea floor. As the sea retreated, the limestone was exposed. The relentless, stormy Southern Ocean and blasting winds gradually eroded the softer limestone, forming caves in the cliffs. The caves eventually became arches and when they collapsed, rock islands up to 45 meters high were left isolated from the shore. The dramatic and imposing limestone cliffs that are the backdrop to the Apostles tower up to 70 meters, while the tallest of the rock stacks is around 45 meters high.

The ebb and flow, the break and crash of each wave against the tall rocks mesmerized me. I think I was unconsciously waiting to see a piece of the rock break off, erode, deteriorate, so that I could say I watched nature in motion. I watched natural history in the present tense. The power of the waves both excited and frightened me. The beauty and the danger were tied inextricably inside my body and mind.

We climbed down in between the cliffs, and the wind had picked up, whipping the orange sand against our faces and in between our clothes. Dropping down seventy meters we stepped into an inlet. The waves were much closer now, more imposing as they beat against the rocks. From the ground, they seemed much higher and foamier. I could hear the salt sizzle as it smashed into the lime-stone. I convinced myself I could hear it crackle on the rocks the way oil burns up in a hot pan. A damp cave had been carved out in the inlet underneath the cliffs, and the more daring of my comrades decided to explore its black nothingness. I waded in a few steps and returned back to sit on the beach and watch the waves come rushing in, filling in all of the gaps between the rocks and the cliffs. I preferred the visible: the blazing hues of the sky and the ocean and the sand.

The group had started to retreat back to the buses. Three hours worth of twenty-five pictures of the same rock had depleted energies and memory cards. I straggled behind, finding a quiet spot to watch the sun begin its descent and the waves continue their struggle against the mighty rocks. There was a calmness, a tranquility that came over me as I sat and let my eyes fix on the slow but powerful water. The colors started to blend, and my eyes watered as the cold wind ravaged my face. I watched the Apostles and tried to imagine their slow formation, but I couldn't. I couldn't begin to understand two million years' worth of nature at work. But I did understand that the change that was happening, however slow, was happening. That change is inevitable. I looked into the sun and knew that in a year I would be looking at the same sun from the other side of the world. I knew that nothing lasts forever, that the time in Australia was precious, and that I had to appreciate everything while I was there.

Back in Baltimore, a little over a year since I left the Twelve Apostles to continue their stoic stances, I looked up at those stars. They were the color of the sky that day on the Great Ocean Road, and feeling the wet rain against my face, I knew that my life was going to change again very soon. Another phase of my life, another trip was ending. But I shouldn't be sad, and I shouldn't worry. E.L. Grant Watson said: "As the waves pass and change, and appear to come again and again to change, they present conflict and adjustment, a duality forming a unity, and a unity, flowing and changing into a manifold destiny."

251

Change intercepts itself. It can be expected or not, but nature allows it to happen so that "what once was" and "what will soon be" crash and diffuse into each other creating "what is." It is a condition of all things natural that we are able to adjust to the things that happen to us. We have the capacity to yield.

The waves that crash against the cliffs and the Twelve Apostles are an ongoing process, a give and take from wave to rock. The phases of one's life are quite like the sand and surf. I know that in a few months I will be out on my own, a change I may or may not be ready for, but I find comfort in the fact that no matter what happens, I will find the calm between the "conflict and adjustment" of my natural life.

The future of publishing...today!

Apprentice House is the country's only campus-based, student-staffed book publishing company. Directed by professors and industry professionals, it is a nonprofit activity of the Communication Department at Loyola College in Maryland.

Using state-of-the-art technology and an experiential learning model of education, Apprentice House publishes books in untraditional ways. This dual responsibility as publishers and educators creates an unprecedented collaborative environment among faculty and students, while teaching tomorrow's editors, designers, and marketers.

Outside of class, progress on book projects is carried forth by the AH Book Publishing Club, a co-curricular campus organization supported by Loyola College's Office of Student Activities.

Student Project Team for *Lavender & Old Ladies:*
> Kevin Zazzali '07
> Jerrell Cameron '07
> Julia Sherrier '08

Eclectic and provocative, Apprentice House titles intend to entertain as well as spark dialogue on a variety of topics.

Financial contributions to sustain the press's work are welcomed. Contributions are tax deductible to the fullest extent allowed by the IRS.

To learn more about Apprentice House books or to obtain submission guidelines, please visit www.ApprenticeHouse.com.

Apprentice House
Communication Department
Loyola College in Maryland
4501 N. Charles Street
Baltimore, MD 21210
Ph: 410-617-5265 • Fax: 410-617-5040
info@apprenticehouse.com